HOW TO EAT LIKE A
REPUBLICAN

HOW TO EAT LIKE A

REPUBLICAN

OR, HOLD THE MAYO, MUFFY—

I'M FEELING MIRACLE WHIPPED TONIGHT

SUSANNE GRAYSON TOWNSEND

ILLUSTRATIONS BY TONY ZAMORA

V   VILLARD | NEW YORK

A Villard Books Trade Paperback Original

Copyright © 2004 by Susanne Grayson Townsend
Illustrations copyright © 2004 by Tony Zamora

Library of Congress Cataloging-in-Publication Data

Townsend, Susanne Grayson.
How to eat like a Republican: or Hold the mayo, Muffy, I'm feeling
Miracle Whipped tonight / Susanne Grayson Townsend; illustrations by Tony Zamora.
p. cm.
ISBN 0-8129-7102-7
1. Cookery.   2. Cookery—Humor.   3. Republican Party (U.S.: 1854–   )—Humor.
I. Title.

TX714.T69 2004
641.5'02'07—dc22
2003065797

Villard Books website address: www.villard.com

Printed in the United States of America on acid-free paper

246897531

For Dad

ACKNOWLEDGMENTS

The thing about the acknowledgments is that no one ever reads them except people who expect to be acknowledged. So unless you have some reason to hope (or fear) that your name will appear here, you're not even reading this at all. Which is too bad, because while it is true that in, say, travel and self-help books, this is where the authors thank their Sherpas and shrinks, and rehabbed movie stars praise the staff and support team at Betty Ford, in cookbooks it's where the steamy sex scenes are. You didn't know that? Ha. I didn't think so.

First of all, I have to thank any and everyone in area code 212 (Verizonspeak for Manhattan) who had anything at all to do with this book. As I mention (okay, okay, *dwell on*) throughout the book, being a Republican in the Pink Apple is, next to the Maytag Repairman's, the Loneliest Job in Town. So to those of you who came out of the closet (if only the linen closet), stepped up to the plate (if only the heirloom Limoges), and stood up to be counted (if only on the fingers of one hand), this book's for you.

Many of you appear in the actual text, attached to your recipes and anecdotes. Others of you contributed in ways only you could: Julie Begel Meyer and Erni Brown, testers and tasters and so much more. Jim Flaherty, Bob Skibsted, Regine and Francois Sicart, Lynnie Giordano, and Mona Mangan, champions and cheerleaders from start to finish. Brilliant Bob Tore, who led me to my agent, the dazzling Jane Dystel. Mary Bahr, editor extraordinaire, tutor, tester too, and friend. Laura Ford, Beth Pearson, Kate Blum, and Tom Perry, the dream team at Random House. The intrepid superintendent, doormen, deskmen, handymen, and porters in my apartment building, who ate their way through most of this book, often at odd times of the day (and night), and were most forthcoming with their opinions and suggestions. Boy, were they ever. West of the Hudson, Jane Andrae Vetter started it all, opening doors while husband Tom opened stone crabs and sauvignon blanc. Mary Ann Azar Allison, my cousin Sheila Sprague, and much of the cast of the 1996 Grayson family reunion are all vividly, if mostly invisibly, represented here.

In fairness, I must mention that the political views of many of these generous individuals do not always reflect those of the management—not by a long shot—but sometimes, like this time, pals trump politics, and I am the richer for it.

Which brings me, here at the very end, to where it all began, and still begins, with Mom. Along with, somewhere in that big Republican Convention in the sky, Dad. Whatever spirit and soul and guts and glory—and goofy—that may have trickled down to us, starts there.

And lastly, a special and heartfelt thanks to every administration, present and past, who have taught me the most valuable lesson of all: In America, you can get away with anything, including a cookbook called *How to Eat Like a Republican*.

CONTENTS

CHAPTER SEVEN

G.O.Peas and Other Chosen Sides

CHAPTER EIGHT

You Can't Make a Bloody Mary Without Breaking Eggs, and Fourteen Other Reasons Republicans Love Brunch

CHAPTER NINE

Unimpeachable Cobblers, or, The Party's Over   *129*

INTRODUCTION

It has been said that Republicans go to the hospital because they love the food.

This is not only unkind, it is untrue.

What hospital in America serves Carl's Famous Night-Before Brunch? Or Evelyn's Pickle-Stuffed Clay Pot Flank Steak? Or Aunt Maxine's Old-Fashioned Vinegar Balls? And when's the last time you got a decent plate of Funeral Chicken on your lunch tray? Not darned likely, missy, not even in a private room.

No, Republicans don't go to the hospital for the food. They go to the country club. Or to fund-raisers. Or to their mother's recipe files—treasured family favorites lovingly handed down from generation to generation, many still on the backs of Bisquick boxes.

Republicans are just like you and me, only with more Tabasco. They make meat loaf just like you and me, only with whiter bread crumbs. They eat sushi just like you and me—no, wait, I take that back.

You will find in these pages a veritable outpouring of Republican recipes, many poured out from a veritable Who's Who of Republican cooks. Sally Danforth's Lemony Hollandaise Sauce. Nancy Lindsay's Spotted Dick Nixon. Irene Halligan's Mighty Mac and Cheese. Pat Buchanan's Buffalo Right Wings. Rush's Mom's Fluffy Potato Casserole.

And you will find some true Republican legends: Magic Never-Fail Christmas Day Roast Beef. Beer-Can Chicken. Amazing Automatic Coconut Cream Pie.

What they share is a love of food and family and old-fashioned flavors, a no-nonsense, cloth-coat sensibility to get dinner on the table—and best of all, they just plain taste good.

FOR THOSE WHO FEEL THEY HAVE RECEIVED
THIS BOOK IN ERROR

Look, we who live to watch Peter Jennings's election-night predictions accept that not everyone in America, let alone Florida, is a Republican. We realize you may have bought this book by accident, or perhaps even received it as a "gag" gift. To that end, I have prepared a useful guide to a more complete understanding and greater enjoyment of the book you now, even if inadvertently, hold in your hands.

Here then, some Frequently Asked Questions about *How to Eat Like a Republican*.

FAQ #1: What in the world is this book about?
How to Eat Like a Republican is part cookbook, part how-to for non-Republicans, part how-come (as in "how come we ever ate that????"), part payback ("thanks, Mom, for all the swell tricks with Lipton Onion Soup Mix"), and part sheer revenge, as in the horrible night a coven of New York Democrats invited innocent people to dinner under the pretext of a whole roasted prime tenderloin, and served instead a whole roasted baby tuna: "Great news! I was walking by Citarella, saw them carrying in this gorgeous thing, and raced home and froze the tenderloin!" My date, a Republican and a fish-hater (a Republican redundancy, by the way; see Chapter 3, "Fish"), memorably reacted by getting dead drunk and passing out at the table with his face in a plateful of the gorgeous thing.

Put another way, *How to Eat Like a Republican* is about food over frou-frou, life before balsamic vinegar, and a growing suspicion that, as a friend of mine once wrote in a heart-wrenching country-and-western anthem: "Just Outside Manhattan, There's a Place Called USA."

And there aren't any New York Democrats there.

FAQ #2: Why on earth would anybody write this book?
I decided to write *How to Eat Like a Republican* because somebody had to, because food should be good, food should be fun, politics are

funny, and Republicans are just plain funnier than Democrats. Unintentionally so, but so. We're just so gosh-darned earnest.

Plus, now that they've pulled this campaign finance reform scam on us, Republicans need all the money they can get. Anybody wanna buy a cookbook?

FAQ #3: Speaking of which, who in Sam Hill would buy a book called How to Eat Like a Republican? *Other than the pervert who bought it for me.* First of all, Republicans. The seven or eight who live in Manhattan, of course (civics lesson: even with Rudy and Mike, registered Democrats in New York City outnumber registered Republicans five to one, or roughly the ratio of women to men on any given Carnival cruise), and the others, the president-electing others, who live everywhere else.

And second, Democrats, especially the self-styled Northeast Cultural Elite, who keep Republicans around for amusement, much as the French kept small playful dogs around, right up to that unpleasant Marie-Antoinette–Louis the Whichever incident.

Both ways, everybody wins, except for anybody who voted for Ross Perot, which is a problem no cookbook can solve, not even mine.

FAQ #4: Where do these wonderful and wonderfully easy recipes come from?

Thanks—I knew you'd come around. The truth is, many of the delectable recipes in *How to Eat Like a Republican* could have come straight out of almost any community cookbook; in fact, I suspect many of them did. My own mother thinks her own Mother's Company Ham Loaf might be from a local cookbook she bought forty years ago in Miami Beach (*Miami Beach???* And that woman is a *Republican!!!!*), but she's not sure; it might be from Aunt Maxine. Either way, it is so sensational, nobody really cares.

And that's the point. Republicans mostly grow up on food that, if it didn't come off a Pillsbury box, somebody just made up one night, usually in a pinch and probably with the aid of a can opener. The family likes it; it gets scribbled down on the back of the telephone bill (or, if the Republican is also a Virgo—a truly troubling thought—tidily inscribed on a lined index card) and then passed around. Some of these recipes remain inviolable, the gospel according to Nobody Remembers Who; others pick up hitchhikers as they make their way around the country with each cook adding her own spin. However they arrive, the ones that survive have earned it, and several have earned their way into *How to Eat Like a Republican*. A dubious distinction perhaps, but this collection is a highly arbitrary one, with me doing all the arbitrating.

One last point: Very *unlike* community cookbooks, whose intentions are invariably virtuous, involving as they do the raising of sums for various charitable institutions (such as the Republican National Committee), *How to Eat Like a Republican* is not high-minded at all. In fact, it's pretty low-minded, once you get into it. Deliciously low-minded, but low-minded just the same.

FAQ #5: I am a Democrat. Will I be insulted by this book?

I certainly hope so. As will some Republicans, as there are individuals on both sides (and You Know Who They Are) still bearing the scars from their Sense of Humorectomies—a sort of comic circumcision many Americans endure at birth. In other words, this book is an equal opportunity offender, albeit with a distinct leaning to the right. *How to Eat Like a Republican* is a celebration of good old-fashioned bipartisan mean-spiritedness, because isn't that the American way, for Pete (Domenici's) sake?

FAQ #6: I am a New Yorker. What does a Republican actually look like?

Hmm, this is a tough one. Because unless you accidentally attend a rally for George Pataki, George Bush, or Georgette Mosbacher, you could easily live a lifetime in the northeast corridor without ever setting eyes on one.

But let me try:

To begin with, while it is true many WASPs (and you do know what they look like, don't you?) are Republicans, many, many more Republicans are not WASPs; Rudy Giuliani, Colin Powell, Arnold Schwarzenegger, Senator Ben Nighthorse Campbell, and Dr. Condoleezza Rice spring to mind. No, most of today's Republicans do not regularly ride to the hounds; they ride to the next tee shot in their own EZ-Gos; or, in some parts of the country, in their Cadillac Escalades to the nearest neighbor, often several hundred thousand acres of good grazing land away.

So you have to be careful. It's not as easy as it used to be, and first thing you know, your daughter comes home from Yale engaged to one, and just like that, *The Nation* won't renew your subscription. Told you she should have gone to Bard.

But it's a good question, and it has prompted me to prepare the following handbook, a special pull-out section to carry with you at all times. Actually, it's more of a rip-out section, as perforations were too expensive for a book this cheap.

REPUBLICANS OF NORTH AMERICA:
A FIELD GUIDE

The Big Fat Rich Republican: the
person whose name is on the brand-
new gym/library/computer center at
the prestigious Ivy League college his
kid just got into, despite a 560 (combined) on his
SATs and an arrest on two counts of possession.

The New Republican: a Democrat who got rich.

The Fake Republican: a Democrat, only a *really* rich one, politically
ambitious but politically unknown, who lives somewhere where
there are wayyyyy too many Democrats seeking public office. He
knows it will be tough to win the primary the old-fashioned way, so
presto-change-o, he becomes a Republican, dodges the primary,
and simply buys the general election.
   Or maybe that *is* the old-fashioned way.

The Stealth Republican: similar to the above, but much cheaper to
pull off. This is a true red-blooded Republican who lives somewhere where there are wayyyyy too many Democrats seeking to
keep Democrats in public office. So he registers as a Democrat and
votes in the Democratic primaries for the lamest possible candidate
in the field, a real loser even a Republican can beat, even in New
York. Don't you just love the two-party system?

The Boy Republican: the brand-new junior partner at the broker-
age/investment banking/real estate firm that, coincidentally, bears
his same last name.

The Girl Republican: the beautiful blond (always) daughter of The
Big Fat Rich or The New Republican. She is pro-choice (usually

choosing Neiman's over Saks, but it depends on the sales), much to the consternation of her parents, but Knows In Her Heart that *so is Laura Bush*. She is the future of the party. Which begins in about half an hour, by the way, and the bouncer at the door is an old boyfriend, so no problemo.

The Movie Star Republican: a very small category, occupied almost entirely by a huge Austrian guy who is married to a skinny little Big Fat Rich Democrat. Go figure.

The Country-and-Western Singing Star Republican: a musical artist of such depth, sensitivity, vulnerability, and originality that he/she is actually invited to perform for the president and first lady of the United States of America at the Kennedy Center in Washington, D.C.
    Just about every Saturday night.

The Temporary Republican: a Democrat from New York, who, for his own safety, puts an American flag in his lapel and an NRA bumper sticker on his rental car as he travels through Arizona and Orange County, California.

The Ex-Republican: rarely sighted, as he usually operates disguised as a U.S. senator, who, in order to thoroughly piss off the Party, hog some headlines, bewilder the people who voted for him, and endear himself to the French, renounces his Republicanism and begins calling himself an Independent, which is Navajo for Democrat. He even votes for the Clinton health-care plan, making him very independent indeed, as even the Democrats didn't.

The Dead Republican: the ex-Republican if Tony Soprano were running the RNC.

HOW TO USE THIS BOOK

.... ★

As most of you will have never before seen a Republican cookbook, at least not knowingly, you may need a little help navigating this one. Please take a moment to scan this section, as it will add immeasurably to the experience.

On the surface, the book is very straightforward, almost childlike in its simplicity. Organized loosely along the lines of a dinner party, recipes for cocktails and appetizers glide gracefully into first courses and main courses, then slide smoothly through side dishes and brunch dishes, concluding pleasantly, if predictably, with desserts. No surprises here. But in the interest of full disclosure, there are some aberrations I feel I must point out: specifically, three close encounters of the Republican kind not present in your average cookbook, and beginning with children.

1. FAVORITE SONS AND DAUGHTERS: *The Care and Feeding of the Republican Acorn*

I tread softly here, as I realize it is a disturbing thought for some people to learn that Republicans actually have children. What's more, they get them the same way non-Republicans do, which is a disturbing thought for some Republicans. But facts are facts, and much as my non-Republican friends might disagree, the little tykes have to eat, so they can grow up healthy and strong and vote a straight party line. So sprinkled here and there you will find some things especially kid-appropriate—yours to embrace or avoid; I leave it to you.

2. COOKIN' WITH COKE: *Pop Culture, Republican Style*

Let's get one thing straight right off the bat: The only thing Republicans put up their noses is ZiCam. So all you body-piercing, tattoo-wearing, dirty-lyrics-writing non-Republicans just back off; our coke has a last name and it's Cola. Therefore, from time to time you will stumble upon an offering or two from a curious subculture of Republicans, those who use soft drinks as a cooking ingredient. It's probably a Southern thing—most scary food things are—but be that as it may, don't sneer until you've tasted Chicken Gizzard Candy with Ketchup and Coke (page 24), Straub's Sticky Chickies in Coke (page 62), St. Bernard's Choca-Cola Cake (page 136), and other carbonated concoctions. All strange but true, and truly, tastily Republican.

And now, the thorniest issue of all, one I have struggled with since the inception of the book:

3. GIVE ME LIBERALS, THEN GIVE ME DEATH
A Short and Highly Selective Sampling of Non-Republican Recipes from Certain Leftward-Leaning Friends Who Demanded Equal Time but Aren't About to Get It

You know who they are. The arugula eaters. The people who buy free-range chicken, prepare their own duck confit, and establish relationships with their fishmongers in order to get first crack at all that fish the Republicans wouldn't touch with a stick. In New York, we call them Democrats. You probably have your own name for them. At any rate, in the interest of still being invited to their dinner parties, I have included a handful of their recherché offerings, such as: William Least Heat-Moon's Pappy Van Winkle on the Rocks (page 7), Magi's Baked Gnocchi (what did I tell you? page 109), my own Aunt Emmy's Bleeding Heart Brownies (page 145; Aunt Emmy still has her 1980 JANE WYMAN WAS RIGHT button pinned to her purse), and a (very) few others.

These and the other recipes in this vein will be clearly and emphatically marked by the symbol shown above. I do not necessarily recommend these contributions, but they are, after long deliberation, included, so do with them what you will.

And now, let's get down to business.

Gentlemen, start your Osterizers.

HOW TO EAT LIKE A
REPUBLICAN

CHAPTER ONE

CHAMPAGNE FINANCE REFORM,
or,
There's No Such Thing as a Free Drink

■■■ ★

PART ONE: COCKTAILS

Let's face it, it's not called the Grand Old for nothing. The Republican *is* the cocktail Party, especially in election years, and isn't it an election year somewhere every year? Not that Democrats don't sip an adult beverage from time to time, but when it comes to Drinking for Dollars, Republicans win by a landslide.

Following are just a few of the many, many delicious cocktails in the Republican oeuvre. Such scope and variety may be daunting to non-Republicans at first ("I only know how to make a plain old vodka and tonic!!!"), but here's a little secret, a *truc* of the trade, if you will: Just double (or triple, or quadruple, you get the idea) the booze, and *voilà,* it's Republican.

In Part Two of this chapter, you will find some simple party-pleasing appetizers, delicious things to do with the hand that's not holding a drink or writing a check. So pass the onion sandwiches, and down the (Orrin) Hatch.

Ooops.

THE GENERAL'S INSTANT MARTINI

This recipe is from Richard M. Connell, Brigadier General, U.S. Army, Ret., whose last assignment was Director of Military Construction, U.S. Army Corps of Engineers, in charge of all construction programs for the Army and the Air Force worldwide. Now obviously, the general was a busy man and devised this recipe because dang it, he just didn't have the *time* to be hunting the danged bottle of vermouth, pulling it out of the danged cabinet, unscrewing the danged cap, and pouring some into the danged glass *every doggoned time he wanted a martini*! I think we can all relate to that. Here is the general's solution.

Take a fresh 1.75-liter (that's a half-gallon in cheap brands) bottle of your favorite gin or vodka and remove the cap. You will notice that before the actual booze begins, there is probably at least a quarter of an inch of perfectly good bottle space simply going to waste. Now. Fill that space with your favorite dry vermouth (this could easily require a teaspoon), replace the cap on the gin, screw on tightly, then shake the bottle to evenly distribute throughout. Place in freezer and Great (George C.) Scott! The perfect martini, about 366 to 1, always ready to serve.

THE BIG APPLETINI

The only hard part here is walking into the liquor store and having to ask for a bottle of the unfortunately named DeKuyper's Pucker Sour Apple Schnapps. Should that indeed prove too daunting, get yourself over to the Society of Illustrators/Museum of American Illustration on East Sixty-third Street in New York and try to wangle your way into the members' bar on the third floor. Michael Sysyn, the club's exceptionally artistic mixologist, makes the best Appletini in town.

> 3 ounces overpriced vodka
> 1 ounce DeKuyper's Pucker Sour Apple Schnapps
> Dash of Lemon-X cocktail mix
> 1 Fred Astaire–type martini glass, chilled until frosty
> 1 thin wedge of New York State Granny Smith green apple, or
>   garnish of your choice (see Note)

Pour the vodka, schnapps, and cocktail mix in a martini shaker with ice and shake for several seconds. Strain into the chilled glass and garnish with the apple wedge.

NOTE: *I once had an otherwise perfectly decent one of these at the Beaver Street Brewery in Flagstaff, Arizona, garnished with a red and green Gummi worm. I rest my case.*

THE CALVIN COOLER

So named for the thirtieth president, who, having made the shrewd decision not to run for reelection in 1928, neatly avoided history's hanging the Great Depression on him. We know of no drink named for Herbert Hoover, his successor, who wound up taking the fall, and who probably could have used that drink a whole hell of a lot more than Cal did.

> 1½ tablespoons fresh lemon juice
> 1½ teaspoons superfine sugar
> 3 ounces (2 jiggers) gin or vodka, or more, to taste
> Ice
> Club soda
> 1 lemon slice, for garnish

In a tall glass, stir together the lemon juice and sugar until the sugar dissolves. Add the gin or vodka and enough ice cubes to fill the glass, and stir. Top off with the club soda, stir again, and garnish with the lemon.

A GOOD OLD-FASHIONED REPUBLICAN OLD-FASHIONED

The perfect beginning for a Good Old-Fashioned Republican Thanksgiving (see page 72).

MAKES 1 DRINK

> 1 sugar cube
> Several dashes of Angostura bitters
> 1 lemon wedge
> 1 orange wedge
> 2 to 4 ounces (you know who you are) Jack Daniel's Black Label, or your favorite bourbon
> Club soda or water
> Cherry, for garnish

Drop the sugar cube into an old-fashioned glass and saturate the sugar with the bitters. Add the lemon and orange wedges and press down with a muddler, a pestle, or the handle end of a dinner knife. Add bourbon, stir well, fill with club soda or water, stir again, and add a cherry for a hypocritical touch of innocence.

THE SALTY YALLER DAWG

A yaller-dawg Democrat, for those of you who bought this book on purpose and for all the Right reasons, is a Democrat who, faced with the option of voting for "an old yaller dog" or a Republican, would vote for the yellow dog. Which is fine with us, because tragically for the DNC, that is so often the case.

2 ounces vodka
2 ounces grapefruit juice

Shake the ingredients over ice cubes in a shaker, strain into a chilled martini glass rimmed with salt, and toast the victorious Republican of your choice.

THE ANEMIC MARY

This recipe is from a bartender at the Admiral's Club at Los Angeles International Airport who would regularly prepare five or six of these for my boss before he (my boss, not the bartender) boarded the eight-A.M. flight back to New York.

MAKES 1 DRINK

8 ounces Beefeater gin
1 ounce Sacramento tomato juice
Ice
1 lime slice
1 celery stalk

Rinse, repeat.
  Bon voyage!

WILLIAM LEAST HEAT-MOON'S PAPPY VAN WINKLE ON THE ROCKS

This recipe, the very first in the book to be marked with the dread Liberal warning, is the creation of William Least Heat-Moon (also creator of *Blue Highways, PrairyErth,* and *River Horse*). It speaks eloquently to the fact that, as I have noted, while posing no threat to Republicans in this arena, occasionally a Democrat will drink, and this recipe is proof—90.4 proof, as a matter of fact.

MAKES 1 DRINK

> Several smooth rocks from the bottom of the Missouri River, washed and placed in the ice cube section of your freezer for a couple of hours. Yes, I know, but stick around; it eventually makes some weird kind of sense.
> 4 ounces Pappy Van Winkle's Family Reserve Bourbon (20 Year)

Select your rocks and put into glass. Add bourbon and enjoy. The drink will stay cold without becoming diluted, which of course is (aha!) the point.

NOTE: *I have successfully prepared this recipe using stones from the Colorado River, Fire Island, Tuckernut Island, Grand Canyon, and even Acapulco Bay, with little discernible difference in the outcome.*

The secret lies in explaining to your cleaning lady why you have a pile of rocks in your freezer before she pitches them.

THE SCOTTSDALE TRILOGY,
or, Who Knew José Cuervo Was a Republican?

(A Short but Educational Detour in Which We Observe the Drinking Rituals of Republican Retirees)

A lot of Republicans are retired, as Republicans, by and large, retire early. Some to minimum-security prisons, to be sure, but usually just because they can, on account of having been the C.E.O. at the time of the hostile takeover.

And while Democrats retire to Florida, Republicans retire to Arizona, or to Rancho Mirage, California. But Arizona is better, because there are even more golf courses, even more Republicans (in California you have to factor in that San Francisco element), and, best of all, almost no fish (see Chapter 3, "Fish").

But just as important, Arizona affords Republicans the chance to expand their culinary horizons, namely to tequila. And it gives them the opportunity to share *con ustedes* (they also pick up some Spanish, in order to banter with the greenskeepers), some *bebidas especiales de los Republicanos de la American Southwest.*

Doesn't Republican sound cute in Spanish?

STEVE'S MARGARITA

First, a word about the Boulders, where Steve works. The Boulders is in Carefree, Arizona, where the thoroughfares have names like Easy Street, Slumber Street, Lazy Lane, Nonchalant Avenue, Rocking Chair Road, and Peaceful Place. The main intersection is where a street named Ho crosses another street named Hum. I do not think this is a coincidence.

The Boulders Club is for the retired captains of industry whose adobe haciendas surround its two eighteen-hole golf courses. It is the kind of club where, upon meeting someone new (a rare event), one asks, "And who did you used to be?" Steve is the head bartender, and therefore, a very popular fellow. Now back to Steve's margarita.

MAKES 1 DRINK

> Iced glass
> 2 lime wedges
> Coarse salt in a flat dish
> 3 parts tequila
> 1 part fresh-squeezed lime juice
> 1 part Cointreau or Triple Sec

Rub the rim of the glass with 1 wedge of lime and swirl the rim into the salt dish. Combine the rest of the ingredients in a blender. Pour into the glass, garnish with the lime, and add ice if desired, but most of Steve's customers aren't those kinds of sissies.

RICK'S EMERGENCY MARGARITA

Rick is my brother, who, while not retired, does play golf and once ran out of limes. Desperate times call for desperate measures; in this case, about 3 to 1.

MAKES 1 DRINK

> ¾ goblet Jose Cuervo
> ¼ goblet Jose Cuervo Margarita Mix

Same nonsense with the glass, lime, and salt as for Steve's Margarita (see above), but you can skip all that if it's a big enough emergency, and by now it probably is.

DAD'S MARGARITA

MAKES 1 DRINK

> 4 ounces Jack Daniel's Black Label
> Ice

(Dad was eighty-one, and set in his ways.)

ROSEMARY'S WALNUTS

These are nice to have on the bar, right by the pledge cards. Make a lot and make ahead, and store them in a Ziploc bag in the freezer. Bring to room temperature before serving, or reheat in the microwave. These are great to have on hand: money in the bank for when thirsty Republicans drop by to give you their money.

MAKES 2 CUPS

> 2 cups walnut halves
> ½ stick (4 tablespoons) unsalted butter, melted
> 1 teaspoon garlic salt
> 1 teaspoon cayenne pepper
> 3 tablespoons chopped fresh rosemary

Preheat the oven to 350°F.

In a large bowl, toss the walnut halves with the remaining ingredients. Spread in one layer on a foil-lined cookie sheet and bake for 20 to 30 minutes, or until browned. Dark brown is good. Or, cook in a dry skillet over medium-high heat, stirring, until browned. Dark brown is still good. Serve warm.

MIMI RAGSDALE'S D.A.R. DEVILED EGGS

Mimi Coffin Ragsdale numbers among her ancestors a passenger on the *Mayflower* and another who founded Nantucket. It should therefore come as no surprise that Mimi's early political influences were fairly specific, beginning with her mother, Martha Gallup Williams Coffin, who refused to buy rolls of fifteen-cent stamps because Franklin Delano Roosevelt's picture was on them.

1 dozen eggs, hard-boiled
⅔ cup Hellmann's mayonnaise, or to taste
2½ teaspoons French's yellow mustard, or to taste
Dash of Tabasco sauce
Dash of garlic salt
Paprika for garnish
Republican (the curly, unfashionable kind) parsley

Halve the eggs lengthwise and remove the yolks to the bowl of a food processor, reserving the whites. Process the yolks with the mayonnaise until smooth and moist, then add the mustard. Taste and add Tabasco and garlic salt. Spoon or pipe (Mimi pipes—she's a Coffin, remember?) the mixture into reserved egg-white halves. Sprinkle paprika over the tops and serve nestled in beds of parsley.

TOM'S TOOTH-ACHIN' BACON

Only Republicans would put brown sugar on bacon and call it food. But I defy you to eat just one of these and ever watch Tom Daschle on C-SPAN again.

Actually, I defy you to eat just one of these, period. Nobody at the Bogey Club in St. Louis, Missouri, has ever been able to since executive chef Tom Elkin invented them in 1976.

MAKES ABOUT 36 PIECES, DEPENDING ON THE THICKNESS OF THE BACON

1 cup brown sugar
$\frac{1}{4}$ cup cinnamon
1 pound bacon

Preheat the oven to 375°F.

In a shallow pan or bowl, mix the brown sugar and cinnamon.

Cut the bacon slices in half crosswise, then roll the slices around in the sugar mixture, pressing until coated. Roll the bacon like a pinwheel and secure with toothpicks. Place, cut side up, on a fine-meshed wire rack that has been placed on a baking sheet (the rack and baking sheet should be lightly coated with oil or sprayed with Pam), or, if the rack isn't fine enough, place a sheet of aluminum foil on it and poke holes for the bacon to drain.

Bake until brown and crispy. Be careful not to burn. Let cool slightly and serve. Go back into the kitchen and make more.

NOTE: *If you leave the bacon slices whole, dredge them in sugar-cinnamon as above, and bake them flat, they make amazin' bacon for a brunch.*

PIG ON A STICK TWO WAYS

Because pork is our friend, here are two more verses of the same great song.

PAVAROTTIS

Twelve 8-inch sesame breadsticks
12 slices prosciutto
1 cup mayonnaise
1 teaspoon Good Seasons salad dressing mix
1 cup grated Parmesan cheese
1 teaspoon oregano

Preheat the oven to 325°F.

Spiral-wrap the sesame breadsticks in the prosciutto, tearing strips if necessary, gently stretcccchhhhing the prosciutto if necessary to cover them top to bottom, and place on a rack set on a foil-lined cookie sheet. Bake for 30 minutes or so, or until the prosciutto is browned.

Meanwhile, stir the salad dressing mix into the mayonnaise, and on a plate, combine the Parmesan and oregano. When the prosciutto is browned, remove it from the oven and immediately roll in the seasoned mayonnaise, then in the Parmesan-oregano mixture. Let cool and serve at room temperature. These can be stored in an airtight container for several days.

SWEET HOT CHILI BACON STICKS

MAKES 12

12 strips bacon
Twelve 8-inch breadsticks (I like sesame here as well, but plain ones are fine, too)
⅓ cup light brown sugar, packed
3 tablespoons hot pure chili powder

Preheat the oven to 350°F.

Stretch and spiral the bacon around the breadsticks from top to bottom. On a plate, combine the brown sugar and chili powder. Roll the breadsticks in the sugar-chili mixture and place on a rack over a foil-lined cookie sheet. Bake for 25 to 30 minutes, or until the sugar is caramelized and the bacon is brown. *Gently* remove the pan from the oven; the bacon sticks will be limp and soggy at first, but when cooled they will harden and become dementedly delicious.

HOW ARE THINGS IN GUACAMOLE?

There is plenty of bad guacamole out there. And plenty of good, mostly down at your favorite Mexican restaurant, which is usually happy to sell you a container. But if it's closed, and your back's to the wall, here is about the best and easiest you will ever make. It comes from a friend of a friend of Sandra Day O'Connor (who, because she is a Supreme Court justice, is of course neither a Republican *nor* a Democrat), so you know it's the goods.

Avocados come in two kinds: the big smooth, smug bright green ones, and the smaller blackish-green, sullen, pimply-skinned ones. You want the latter, because they actually taste like avocados. Serrano chiles are smaller than jalapeños, but hotter.

3 ripe avocados
2 to 3 tablespoons fresh lime juice (in a pinch, use lemon juice)
1 serrano chile, minced, or 1 jalapeño
¼ cup chopped onion
2 garlic cloves, minced
1 small ripe tomato, juiced and chopped
¼ cup chopped fresh cilantro, plus more to taste
1 teaspoon salt, plus more to taste

Cut the avocados in half lengthwise, twist to loosen the pit, then take out the pit and give it to your kids to go grow an avocado plant (see Note).

Scoop out the avocado pulp. Use a fork to mash with the remaining ingredients until well combined, but still lumpy. Let stand a bit, then correct the seasoning and serve with tortilla chips, for which an actual recipe for homemade follows, believe it or not.

NOTE: *To grow an avocado plant, stick three toothpicks around the middle of the avocado pit, like a horizontal tripod. Place it fatter side down (where the dark indentation is), pointier side up, in a glass nobody ever uses, balancing it on the rim with the toothpicks. Fill the glass with water halfway up the seed. Soon it will start to sprout, eventually growing into a spindly, useless plant that will initially delight your children, then bore them to beyond. Discard, along with glass (unless there is a someone you need to get even with, say, someone who voted for Hillary in New York, in which case you should save the glass and serve that person a nice big iced tea in it).*

THE ANAL-COMPULSIVE'S HOMEMADE TORTILLA CHIPS, or, Who Knew Martha Stewart Was Mexican?

Y ou don't have to make your own. You really don't. The ones in the bag are perfectly fine, if not as fresh and toasty as these. But if some day, for some reason, you decide you simply must, right after you've alphabetized the contents of your refrigerator and before you découpage the toaster oven, here's how.

MAKES 72 CHIPS (HOW'S THAT FOR ANAL-COMPULSIVE ACCURACY?)

1 dozen corn tortillas
1 skilletful of hot vegetable oil, about 1 inch deep
Salt, for sprinkling

Take a stack of tortillas and a sharp knife, and slice the tortillas into sixths, i.e., Doritos-size wedges. Heat the oil in the skillet to about 375°F., or until a drop of water makes the hot oil spatter angrily, usually right in your face.

Fry the tortilla wedges in batches (now would be a good time to dig down and find the old spatter screen) until toasty-looking; remove to paper towels to drain and dry, and sprinkle with salt. Store in an airtight container if there are any left over, which there probably won't be.

NOTE: *A nice variation is to sprinkle on ground cumin or chili powder with the salt.*

DEEP-DISH NACHO PIE

I have no recollection whatsoever of where I first encountered this recipe, but it is a mainstay in the Midwest and Southwest of any gathering of eight or more margarita drinkers. Though I always considered it strictly the province of the provinces (read Red Neck, White Socks, and Blue Ribbon Beer), it turns out to be one of the most ubiquitous in the book, its most improbable sighting to date having been at a recent gathering of the Northeast Cultural Elite on Manhattan's Upper West Side. There, in an antiques-filled, twelve-room, prewar apartment with fourteen-foot ceilings and views of the Hudson River and the Cathedral of St. John the Divine, it sat, a homely little casserole with chips sticking out of it, amid the caviar, foie gras, and baked Brie—that is, until a pack of really thin people wearing black pounced on it and completely devoured it right before my Republican wide eyes. In other words, stop whatever you are doing and make this right now. In certain circles, like even yours, ten bucks says it can pass for dinner.

SERVES 12, AT LEAST

In an 8 × 12-inch baking dish, layer in this order:

> Two 16-ounce cans refried beans (with chorizo or not, but chorizo is better)
> 1 pound ground beef, cooked with packaged Old El Paso taco seasoning (see the package directions) and 1 chopped onion, and drained of fat
> One 8-ounce package shredded Monterey Jack and Cheddar combo
> One 10-ounce can red enchilada or taco sauce

Bake for 20 minutes at 350°F., remove and let cool, then start layering again:

> 2 cups guacamole (store-bought, local Mexican restaurant–bought, or—sigh—homemade; see page 15)
> 2 cups sour cream
> One 6-ounce can black olives, sliced
> 6 scallions, chopped
> One 4-ounce jar canned pimientos, chopped
> Chopped canned jalapeños, lots for me, you decide for you
> Chopped fresh cilantro (if you can't find it, you'll never miss it—use parsley, or blow the whole green thing off entirely)

> Tortilla chips
> Store-bought salsa

Now. Start sticking tortilla chips, porcupine style, into the top, as many as will fit. Serve extra chips, extra jalapeños, and salsa on the side.

VEL-VETO POWER RO★TEL DIP

This is absolutely disgusting.

But let's begin at the beginning. RO★TEL tomatoes are a special spicy canned tomato for which there is no exact substitute. If you live east of the Mississippi, you may have to goose up normal canned tomatoes with some onion, garlic, and hot chiles, which is not the same, but it's better than going without. This is a big sodden sludge of pure protein, and it is one of the few dishes with which a bag of Tostitos, Doritos, or even Fritos is far more appropriate than the more refined homemade tortilla chips described on page 16.

In other words, this is junk food of the lowest order. And absolutely, positively addictive.

SERVES 12 OR MORE

> 1 pound Velveeta Pasteurized Prepared Cheese Product (see what I'm saying?), broken into melting-size pieces
> One 10-ounce can RO★TEL Tomatoes & Green Chilies (sic)

Combine the cheese and tomatoes in a medium saucepan and stir over low heat until the cheese is melted. Or microwave in a glass bowl, covered, for about 5 minutes, stirring halfway through. Serve with chips, or, in an act of pure self-delusion, raw vegetables.

But wait, there's more: You can also brown a pound of ground beef with some chopped onion and garlic, *then* add the Velveeta and tomatoes and cook until the cheese is melted and the whole thing is one big molten, magnificent mess. Add some Tabasco, then pour into a big bowl and watch your friends make politically incorrect fools of themselves. Honestly, sometimes I hate myself.

THE POLISH REPUBLICAN WITH CRAZY MARY'S MUSTARD SAUCE

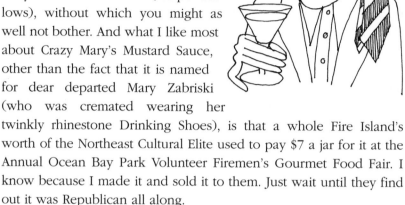

To be perfectly frank about these franks, what's best about them is Crazy Mary's Mustard Sauce (recipe follows), without which you might as well not bother. And what I like most about Crazy Mary's Mustard Sauce, other than the fact that it is named for dear departed Mary Zabriski (who was cremated wearing her twinkly rhinestone Drinking Shoes), is that a whole Fire Island's worth of the Northeast Cultural Elite used to pay $7 a jar for it at the Annual Ocean Bay Park Volunteer Firemen's Gourmet Food Fair. I know because I made it and sold it to them. Just wait until they find out it was Republican all along.

SERVES 8 TO 12

> 1 Hillshire Farms Smoked Polska Kielbasa (the Lite variety works
>   okay here, but the Turkey just doesn't cut it)
> 1 cup fresh lemon juice
> ¼ cup dried oregano
> Freshly ground black pepper
> 24 tiny new potatoes, or 12 larger ones, halved or quartered
>   (optional)
> 2 recipes Crazy Mary's Mustard Sauce (recipe follows)

Slice the sausage into 24 one-bite chunks. Place in a plastic bag with the lemon juice, oregano (rubbed between your hands to release all flavor), and pepper. Marinate in the refrigerator for 1 hour or overnight. Dump everything (including the potatoes, if using) into an oven-friendly casserole, cover, and bake at 350°F. for 1 hour. Serve in the casserole with toothpicks and the sauce.

CRAZY MARY'S MUSTARD SAUCE

MAKES ABOUT 1 1/3 CUPS, BUT TRIPLING IT MAKES
4 CUPS, AND YOU MIGHT AS WELL BECAUSE YOU
WILL USE IT ON EVERYTHING.

    1 tablespoon butter
    1 egg
    3 tablespoons dry mustard powder
    1 tablespoon Grey Poupon, or any Dijon mustard
    3 tablespoons brown sugar
    3 tablespoons white sugar
    1 teaspoon paprika
    1/2 cup cider vinegar
    4 to 5 drops of Tabasco sauce

Melt the butter in a saucepan while you beat together the remaining ingredients. Blend this mixture into the butter and cook
over low heat for 5 minutes, stirring. Let cool. Serve with anything, especially things porcine, like that spiral-cut baked ham
you ordered from the deli and are passing off as your own.

THAT CRAB DIP AGAIN

So named for the charismatic concoction that followed everybody around, cocktail party to cocktail party, for more years than anybody cared to remember, and which now tastes good all over again.
Canned or pasteurized fresh crab meat is okay, as long as it is first
quality.

MAKES ABOUT 2 CUPS

    One 8-ounce package cream cheese
    6 ounces good crab meat, picked over and any little bits of shell
        and cartilage discarded
    1 tablespoon finely chopped onion

½ teaspoon cream-style horseradish
¼ teaspoon salt
Dash of freshly ground black pepper
Dash of Worcestershire sauce
⅓ cup toasted slivered almonds or chopped toasted pecans

Preheat the oven to 375°F.

In a large bowl, combine all the ingredients except the nuts and mix well. Spoon into an 8-inch pie pan or similar dish. Sprinkle the top with the nuts. Bake for 15 minutes. To serve, spread on sturdy crackers.

ELSIE'S BIG HOT CHEESE GOOEY

Think of this not as an oinky, oozing mass of unbridled unctuosity, but as a perfectly sensible addition to your Atkins Diet. I believe this is the only recipe in the book, and maybe in the world, that starts out with two cups of Miracle Whip. Gets your attention, doesn't it?

By the way, this is a recipe that takes terrifically to tinkering: Add chopped jalapeños, cumin, and garlic, serve with tortilla chips, and call it Mexican; or make with bleu cheese and serve with toasted garlic-rubbed baguette toasts and call it French. Make it Elsie's or make it yours, but don't make it for your cardiologist.

SERVES 8 TO 10

2 cups Miracle Whip or mayonnaise
8 ounces Cheddar cheese, grated
2 bunches scallions, chopped
1 red bell pepper, chopped
2 teaspoons Tabasco sauce, plus more to taste
2 teaspoons Worcestershire sauce
Paprika for sprinkling

Preheat the oven to 350°F.

In a large bowl, mix everything together, then spoon into any baking dish big enough to hold it. Smooth out the top and sprinkle with paprika. Bake for 30 minutes, or until golden and bubbling. Let cool until set up a bit, then serve with crackers or seasoned flatbread, if you are not carbophobic, or with virtuous raw vegetables if you are (or just a big spoon and a Danielle Steele novel—author's choice).

ORRIN'S ONION SANDWICHES

This makes as many as you want—and you probably ought to make a lot more than you think you want.

SERVES 6, MAYBE

> 24 slices very thin bread or brioche
> 1 cup good mayonnaise
> 1 bunch of parsley (flat-leaf or Republican curly), chopped
> Softened unsalted butter
> 24 thin, thin slices of onion—red, white, or Vidalia—or slanty-sliced
> scallions

Make bread rounds by stacking slices of the bread and cruelly jamming a biscuit cutter down through them. (Does anyone have a biscuit cutter anymore? No? Then use an empty can from frozen orange juice.) Bam, bread rounds.

Place the mayonnaise and parsley on separate saucers.

Butter one bread round, lay a thin same-size round of sliced onion on it, and top with another bread round. Roll the sandwich edges in the mayonnaise, pinwheel style, then in the parsley. Repeat until all the rounds are used, arranging them smugly on a pretty plate. Cover with a slightly damp towel and refrigerate for 1 hour or more. Serve chilled.

CHICKEN GIZZARD CANDY WITH KETCHUP AND COKE

This is one of those dishes I warned you about, a product of the cult of Coca-Cola Cookery, whose roots are probably in voodoo, or at least Atlanta. This version of Coke Barbecue Sauce is a gift from me to you—one you will thank me for, believe it or not—and if you've never eaten chicken gizzards (except those traveling incognito in giblet gravy), it's a revelation: People gobble these up like, well, candy. Very chewy candy, by the way, so be prepared.

SERVES 6 TO 8

1 pound chicken gizzards (sometimes mixed with hearts, and that's fine—use both)

COKE BARBECUE SAUCE

1 tablespoon oil, or half oil and half butter
1 medium onion, chopped
3 garlic cloves, smashed and chopped
1 cup Coca-Cola
1 cup ketchup
1/4 cup Lea & Perrins Worcestershire sauce, regular or white
Several dashes of liquid smoke
Big pinch of onion powder, or granulated onion
Big pinch of garlic powder, or granulated garlic
1 or 2 canned chipotle peppers, chopped, or 1/2 teaspoon hot red pepper flakes

Preheat the oven to 500°F.

Cut the gizzards in half (hearts can be left whole). Set aside while you make the barbecue sauce.

Heat the oil in a large sauté pan and sauté the onion and garlic until just starting to soften, then dump in all the other ingredients and stir well. Bring to a boil over medium heat, then reduce the heat to a simmer. Cook until the sauce is reduced a bit, 7 to 8 minutes. Stir frequently; don't let it burn. Let cool.

Toss the gizzards with the barbecue sauce until well coated. Spread out on flat baking pan that has been lined with foil, then spoon a bit more sauce over. Bake for 25 to 30 minutes, or until the gizzards are cooked through and the edges are crispy. Serve warm or at room temperature, with toothpicks and more barbecue sauce on the side.

NOTE: *This sauce is fabulous for ribs, chicken, shrimp, anything, and will keep forever in the fridge. Not that it will get the chance.*

CHAPTER TWO

THE PRIMARIES:
First Courses and Salads

The First Course is important to Republicans for two reasons: One, it presumes everybody has already had several cocktails so can now lurch to the dinner table and switch to wine, and two, it gives the hostess the opportunity to use all the oddly shaped dishes and funny forks that Mother stuck her with when she and Dad sold the big house in Greenwich and bought the condo in Carefree.

Now, let's address the salad issue. The Northeast Cultural Elite, and the French, of course, eat salad after the main course, but Republicans think that's un-American. We like our salad first and we like it cold, and we probably won't use mesclun because it sounds prissy, and we won't use extra-virgin olive oil because it sounds dirty. So while these salads are not particularly subtle, they are delicious and time-honored, most dating somewhere around the middle of the Eisenhower administration.

Oh, and if it's a really special occasion, we may even chill the plates and forks, just like at the Club.

IRENE HALLIGAN'S SHRIMP AND RASPBERRY HARICOTS VERTS

rene Halligan was New York City Chief of Protocol and Commissioner to the United Nations and Consular Corps (whew!) during the Giuliani administration, which, translated, means she was pretty much first lady much of that time. She is currently first vice chairman of the New York Republican County Committee, a Mayor Bloomberg–appointed member of the host committee for the 2004 Republican National Convention, and a delegate to same. Oh, and past president of the Women's National Republican Club. Now, you may look at that résumé and then at that haricots verts stuff, and decide that maybe Irene has gotten just a liiiittle too big for her britches, but you would be wrong. Just flip to Irene Halligan's Mighty Mac and Cheese (page 80) and you will see that even though somebody taught her a fancy-shmancy word for little skinny green beans one time, she is still my down-to-earth pal from the seventies she's always been. And one terrific cook.

SERVES 4

> 1½ pounds medium shrimp, peeled and deveined
> 8 ounces haricots verts (those skinny little green beans discussed above)
> 3 tablespoons chopped chives
> Grated zest of 1 small orange
> 1 teaspoon freshly ground black pepper, plus more to taste
> 2 tablespoons raspberry vinegar
> 1 teaspoon Dijon mustard
> Salt to taste
> ⅓ cup mild olive oil
> 1 cup fresh raspberries
> 1 bunch of watercress, trimmed

In a large pot of lightly salted boiling water, boil the shrimp for 1 minute; drain and cool. In a separate pot of boiling water, blanch the beans for 1 minute; plunge them into ice water, drain, and pat dry. Toss the shrimp and beans together and gently add 2 tablespoons of the chives, the orange zest, and the pepper.

president of the United States on the Prohibition Ticket, coming in fourth to Dwight D. Eisenhower in the national election. I am relieved to report that by the time I met him, in 1971, he had clearly rethought the mission statement of that party, and had in fact embraced the instruments of its inevitable demise.

But about that soup . . .

SERVES 6

1 cup chunky peanut butter
3 cups beef broth
1 bunch of scallions, trimmed and coarsely chopped
2 cloves garlic
1½ cups half and half
2 teaspoons cumin
1 teaspoon chili powder
1 teaspoon Tabasco
½ cup white wine
3 tablespoons red wine vinegar
Salt and pepper to taste

In a blender, puree the peanut butter, 1 cup of the beef broth, the scallions, and the garlic. Pour into a saucepan and add the remaining beef broth and the half and half, cumin, chili powder, and Tabasco. Bring to a boil, reduce the heat, and simmer 15 minutes. Add the white wine, red wine vinegar, salt, and pepper and simmer 5 minutes more. Serve hot or cold, garnished with chopped scallions or radishes, cubed avocado bits, and croutons, in semi-hollowed-out avocado halves. (I'm not kidding. She really did.)

BOB AND JANE TAYLOR'S ARDSHEAL STILTON SOUP

So here's the story: I have these friends who had great big fancy jobs in New York in banking and advertising, respectively, a town house in the city and a country house upstate, and two kids enrolled in a top Manhattan private school attended by others of their kind, the (all together now) Northeast Cultural Elite . . . who one day, on a family trip to Scotland, came across a rambling ramshackle seventeenth-century Stewarts of Appin manor house and said, "Hey, here's an idea: Why don't we quit our jobs, sell the house, disrupt our lives, and move to Scotland and turn this into a five-star country hotel?" And you know what? They did. Ardsheal House became a must-stay for everyone traveling in the Western Highlands, with hostelry and culinary awards by the lorryload, and this simple and simply incredible soup is one of the reasons why.

SERVES 8

    2 tablespoons butter
    1/4 cup finely chopped onion
    1 teaspoon finely minced garlic
    1/2 pound Stilton cheese, crumbled
    1/2 pound Cheddar cheese, grated
    1/3 cup flour
    3 cups chicken broth
    1 cup heavy cream
    1/3 cup dry white wine
    1 bay leaf
    Salt and freshly ground black pepper to taste

Melt the butter in a saucepan and add the onion and garlic. Cook, stirring, until the vegetables are wilted. Add the cheeses and sprinkle with the flour, stirring. Cook, stirring, for about 2 minutes. Gradually add the chicken broth, cream, and wine. Add the bay leaf, salt, and pepper. Bring slowly to a boil. Lower the heat and simmer for 15 to 20 minutes. Remove the bay leaf. If desired, thin with a little milk.

NOTE: *This soup may be made ahead of time, then reheated and thinned if desired.*

OHHHHHHHH!!!KLAHOMA ROASTED ASPARAGUS WITH TANGERINE DRESSING

This is pretty highfalutin stuff from the Dust Bowl, but just wait'll you taste Senator Don Nickles's soigné signature dish. Boomer Sooner!

SERVES 4

1 pound asparagus, ends trimmed, but not peeled
1 tablespoon extra-virgin olive oil
2 large tangerines (or small oranges, but then you have to change the name)
1/2 cup fresh tangerine (or orange) juice
3/4 teaspoon minced peeled fresh ginger
2 teaspoons rice wine vinegar, unseasoned
1 1/2 teaspoons oriental sesame oil (the dark kind)
1 garlic clove, pressed
Salt and freshly ground pepper
2 tablespoons finely chopped scallion tops (the green part)
2 tablespoons finely chopped dry-roasted peanuts

Preheat the oven to 450°F. while you soak the asparagus in cold water to cover for 15 minutes. Drain and spread in a 13 × 9 × 2-inch baking pan; drizzle with the olive oil. Roast the asparagus until crisp-tender, turning occasionally, about 10 minutes. Transfer to a platter and cool.

Grate the tangerine zest and reserve 1 1/2 teaspoons. Using a sharp knife, remove the rest of the peel and white pith from the fruit. Cut between the membranes to release the segments. Arrange the segments atop the asparagus.

In a small bowl, whisk the tangerine juice, the reserved zest, the ginger, vinegar, sesame oil, and garlic to blend. Season the dressing with salt and pepper to taste; drizzle over the asparagus. Sprinkle with the scallion tops and peanuts and serve.

THE SENATOR'S SALAD

I actually am in possession of a photograph of the Honorable John C. Danforth, Jr., breaking an egg over this salad, in a very non-senatorial moment. It is in a little cookbook his wife, Sally, wrote way back when Jack was attorney general of the state of Missouri. If you know someone who was on their Christmas card list around 1969 and received it, do whatever it takes to get your hands on it. Sally Danforth's cookbook is a tiny treasure, and she has been most generous in sharing its recipes.

SERVES 6 TO 8, GENEROUSLY

Soak 2 garlic cloves in ¼ cup olive oil overnight. Cube 5 pieces of bread and toast the cubes on a baking sheet in a 300°F. oven until brown (makes 2 cups).

Break up 2 heads of romaine or iceberg lettuce in a salad bowl. Put over the top ½ cup grated Parmesan cheese, ¼ cup crumbled blue cheese, ½ teaspoon salt, and ½ teaspoon freshly ground black pepper. Drizzle on 6 tablespoons of the garlic oil along with 3½ tablespoons lemon juice and 1 tablespoon Worcestershire sauce. Break a raw egg over the top.

Drizzle the rest of the garlic oil over the croutons and toss, then add to the salad.

MAYA SCHAPER'S BLEU TIPPECANOES WITH SHERRY VINAIGRETTE

Maya Schaper owns a magical shop on Manhattan's Upper West Side called Maya Schaper's Cheese and Antiques. Retro-fitted, it performed as the sweet little neighborhood bookstore Meg Ryan owned and defended against Tom Hanks's big mean bully bookstore in the movie *You've Got Mail*. So far so good. However, as it is almost certain Maya is the only Republican on the Upper West Side, I can only be happy she has long since collected her lavish location fee, as I am pretty sure neither Meg Ryan nor Tom Hanks is a Republican.

Use the pointy white torpedo-shaped endive here, not the curly leafy kind.

SERVES 4 TO 6

> 2 heads endive
> ½ pound real Roquefort or really good blue cheese, softened
> 1 cup skillet-toasted walnuts, chopped
> Sherry Vinaigrette, or Dee Austin's Maple Syrup Vinaigrette
>   (recipes follow)

Chop the stubby ends off the endives, and start separating the leaves into little endive canoes. When you can't separate any more leaves, chop off the next stubby end, and continue as above. When the canoes are all made, spoon cheese into each and divide evenly among small plates, arranging artfully in a Junior League sort of way. Sprinkle the walnuts around and pour the dressing over. The Junior League would serve these with dainty knives and forks, naturally, but I prefer them as finger food.

SHERRY VINAIGRETTE

> 2 teaspoons Dijon mustard
> 2 tablespoons sherry vinegar
> 2 tablespoons chopped scallions
> 6 tablespoons extra-virgin olive oil
> Salt and freshly ground black pepper to taste

Whisk all the ingredients together in a small bowl.

DEE AUSTIN'S MAPLE SYRUP VINAIGRETTE

¾ cup Wesson oil
¼ cup red wine vinegar
1 garlic clove, smashed and minced
1 chopped shallot
¼ cup country-style mustard
½ cup pure maple syrup
Salt and freshly ground black pepper
Big dash of Tabasco sauce

Whisk all the ingredients together in a medium bowl.

TOM'S ARTICHOKE TOASTS IN THE GARDEN

Tom Elkin has been creating these (and everything else edible) for the Bogey Club in St. Louis since 1976. Without the salad, you can put them on a platter and pass them at a cocktail party. Or put a big plate of them beside the Drunken Crabs (page 48) and watch the deliriously depraved among your guests use them for dunking in the broth.

MAKES ABOUT 30 PIECES

1 French bread baguette, sliced about ⅜ inch thick
1 garlic clove, cut in half
2 tablespoons olive oil, plus more for brushing on the toasted
    bread
Two 14-ounce cans artichoke hearts (not marinated), drained and
    squeezed dry in a kitchen towel
½ medium onion, diced
2 celery stalks, diced
1 hefty tablespoon crushed and minced garlic
¼ cup mayonnaise

¼ cup roasted red bell pepper, diced (your own, or good canned ones)

½ cup freshly grated Parmesan cheese

Salt and freshly ground black pepper to taste

2 bunches of watercress tossed with your favorite simple vinaigrette

Preheat the oven to 350°F.

Place the bread slices on a baking sheet and toast in the oven until crispy and almost dry. While hot, rub with the cut garlic, then brush with olive oil and set aside.

Chop the artichokes by hand or in a food processor until very fine.

Sauté the onion and celery in the 2 tablespoons olive oil until almost translucent. Add the garlic and warm slightly. Place into a mixing bowl and add all the other ingredients except the watercress. Mix well. The texture should be smooth and creamy, but not too moist. If too moist, add a little more Parmesan.

Spread the mixture generously on the toasts and place in the oven to heat through, 10 to 15 minutes; then serve on individual plates of dressed watercress.

MAYFAIR HOTEL DRESSING

Anyone who worked in downtown St. Louis in the forties, fifties, or sixties knew that the Mayfair Hotel was famous for two things, and this was the other one.

MAKES 1 QUART

2 celery stalks, coarsely chopped

1 small onion, coarsely chopped

One 2-ounce can anchovies, drained

1 cup salad oil

3 egg yolks

1 teaspoon dry mustard

1 tablespoon prepared mustard

1 teaspoon garlic powder

Freshly ground black pepper to taste

6 to 8 drops of Tabasco sauce, or to taste
2 tablespoons vinegar, white or cider (nothing too fancy)

Blend the celery, onion, anchovies, and oil in a blender until smooth. Add the remaining ingredients and continue to blend for several seconds. Chill before serving to thicken.

Toss with sturdy greens, like romaine, or make Salad in a Glass: Pour an inch or so of the chilled dressing into the bottoms of as many tall goblets as you have people, and stand romaine leaves, endive spears, scallions, and red bell pepper strips in it, arranging so that the leaves poke up perkily and their bottoms are in the dressing. Eat with your fingers, as you go. So, so good.

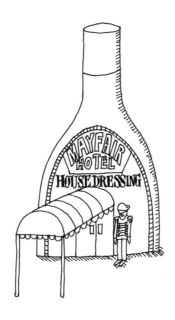

CHARCOAL HOUSE SALAD

Anyone living in suburban St. Louis in the forties, fifties, and sixties will be delighted to know that the Charcoal House still exists, completely and totally intact, down to the red-flocked wallpaper and fried chicken livers. Wanda and George, alas, have departed, first to divorce court, then finally to God's Great Charcoal Grill Up There, but Steak By George and the signature house salad remain. Although they're not on the menu, if you are a regular, you can get a few anchovies piled on top, too.

I don't mean to sound preachy, but every Republican should have the fixins for this salad in the refrigerator at all times.

MAKES 1 QUART DRESSING

DRESSING

1 cup brown sugar
1 cup vinegar
1 cup salad oil
1 cup water
1 tablespoon prepared mustard (that's French's yellow to you, son)
1 garlic clove, sliced lengthwise, to leave in the jar

Iceberg lettuce
Blue cheese, for crumbling
Anchovies, optional

Combine all the dressing ingredients in a screw-top jar, shake well, and let stand overnight. Pour the dressing over iceberg wedges topped by lots of crumbled blue cheese and the anchovies if using.

SIZZLING PINE NUT SALAD

This is a way to bring a whole sexy smoky something to an otherwise routine green salad. It's more method than recipe, so anything you want to throw in after the initial shock-and-awe phase is up to you. And yes, it also works with skillet-toasted dry-roasted peanuts, walnuts, or whatever nut you currently love.

6 SERVINGS

4 tablespoons extra-virgin olive oil (you can borrow this and the balsamic vinegar from the Democrats next door)
2 tablespoons balsamic vinegar
1 fat garlic clove, minced
1 small red onion, sliced thin
1/2 red bell pepper, chopped (optional)
Several thin shavings of Parmigiano-Reggiano cheese (optional)
1/4 cup pine nuts (pignolis)
Mixed salad greens for 6
Salt and freshly ground black pepper to taste

Pour the olive oil and vinegar into a salad bowl. Add the garlic, onion, red pepper, and Parmigiano, if using, and let soak while you fix dinner.

When it's time to serve, heat a small heavy skillet and pour in the pine nuts. Brown the nuts over high heat, shaking the skillet, until they are pretty much burned. When they get to that half-golden, half-black state, take them off the heat and immediately dump them into the salad bowl. They will sizzle and exude a wonderful aroma. At that point, add the salad greens (one of those Liberal-loving mesclun mixtures is allowed here, and actually preferred) and toss. Taste and add salt, and more oil or vinegar if needed, and pass the pepper mill.

FREG AND PED'S CHEATIN' HEART SESAME SALAD DRESSING

A lot of flavor bang for almost no calorie buck. The Czufins (Freg and Ped) are among my oldest and dearest friends—the kind of friends with whom I can discuss anything in the world, everything under the sun, whatever is in my heart. Except politics.

> One 10-ounce bottle Seasoned Rice Wine Vinegar
> 2 to 3 teaspoons toasted sesame oil (the dark Asian kind)

Open the bottle of vinegar and pour in the sesame oil. Shake and taste, and add more sesame oil if you think it needs it. That's the whole recipe. Keep in the fridge forever, to sprinkle over (after vigorous shaking again) romaine lettuce, tarted up with toasted dry-roasted peanuts and chopped scallions or toasted walnuts with bits of blue cheese.

EVELYN GRAYSON'S FOO YUNG TOSS

This salad was my first introduction to the nuances and complexities of fine Chinese cuisine, and it still remains a source of some exotica to Republicans in certain swing states.

This makes enough dressing for three or four of these salad events, so stick the rest in the fridge right next to the Charcoal House Salad dressing (see page 38). The dressing is great with fresh spinach as well, only then Evelyn (a.k.a. Mom) calls it Scrumptious Spinach Salad. Republicans like to name their food.

1 head romaine lettuce, torn into bite-size pieces
One 1-pound can bean sprouts, drained
One 5-ounce can sliced water chestnuts
5 slices crisp-fried bacon, crumbled
2 hard-boiled eggs, sliced
Salt and freshly ground black pepper
1 cup salad oil
½ cup sugar
⅓ cup ketchup
¼ cup cider vinegar
2 tablespoons grated onion
2 teaspoons Worcestershire sauce

In a salad bowl, combine the romaine, bean sprouts, water chestnuts, bacon, and eggs. Sprinkle lightly with salt and pepper. Combine the remaining ingredients in a blender, then pour enough over the salad to dress it completely.

FISH

▪▪ ★

To tell the truth, Republicans don't much like fish.

SEAFOOD

● ★

While it is true Republicans don't much like fish, they do like seafood, especially when it's shrimp and especially when it's free. This happens most frequently at lavish Republican weddings (also known as Mergers & Acquisitions), the openings of Republican presidential libraries, and the dedication of Republican-donated wings to the Mayo Clinic (the one in Scottsdale, naturally, not the one in Hubert Humphrey–happy Minneapolis).

Perhaps more easily accessed, if you know any Republican mothers, are the seafood extravaganzas that occur in country clubs all over Republican America every Mother's Day. And incidentally, if any of you out there think Republicans are not athletic, you obviously have not witnessed the scrimmage following the snap from center at the carved ice swan buffet table holding all those free* shrimp, lobsters, oysters, clams, and stone-crab claws.

---

*Free, as has been elsewhere noted, is in the wallet of the beholder, and perhaps never more so than here, where, if one cared to cavil, one might factor in the club initiation fees, the annual dues, the price of a guest's round of golf, and the assessment for the custom-designed rug in the main dining room that nobody but the rug committee likes. All of which works out to about $300 per free shrimp.

MISSOURI CURRY

This only rhymes if you live in St. Louis or Kansas City, or certain neighborhoods in Springfield where people put on airs. Everybody else in the state knows it is pronounced "Missourah," but "Missourah Currah" is even farther away from Calcutta. Doesn't matter; with enough garnishes (see the end of the recipe), you can entertain Merchant *and* Ivory, and maybe even Helena Bonham Carter, and not have to sit through one of their movies.

This is the very first dish I learned to make for dinner parties, if you don't count Kraft Tangy Italian Spaghetti Dinner or Ramos Gin Fizzes. Hello, Delhi.

SERVES 4 TO 6

¾ stick (6 tablespoons) butter or margarine

6 tablespoons flour

2 to 3 tablespoons curry powder

Pinch of turmeric (I added this touch after I moved to New York and found out what turmeric was; you can skip it if you don't know or care what turmeric is)

One 1-ounce package Lipton Onion Soup Mix

2 cups applesauce

2 cups water

3 tablespoons lemon juice

Several drops of Tabasco sauce (for me, that's about 20, but you can start small and work your way up)

3 cups or more shrimp, peeled and deveined and poached for 1 to 2 minutes (it will cook more in the mixture); or the same amount of leftover roast lamb, chicken, or turkey

Cooked rice

Melt the butter in a large skillet over medium heat. Sauté the flour and curry powder in the melted butter until the curry smells fragrant and the flour is lightly browned. Add everything else but the shrimp. Cook, stirring constantly, over medium heat until thickened (careful, this burns easily), then add the shrimp and heat through.

Serve over cooked rice and with any or all (or none, but you'll be sorry and so will Ismail and James and Helena) of the following condiments, each in its own little bowl you will have to wash later, but it's definitely worth it:

Major Grey's (or anybody else's) chutney
toasted coconut
chopped onion and/or scallion
chopped red and/or green bell pepper
raisins (soaked in rum)
crumbled crisp bacon
chopped hard-boiled egg
chopped roasted (and skillet-toasted, if you like) peanuts
sour cream
pickled melon rind
tomato relish and/or pickle relish
canned chopped pimiento
sautéed sliced banana
mustard pickle
onion relish
Durkee's canned French-fried onions (toasted in a skillet and
highly recommended)
Bombay Duck, toasted and crumbled, which is a really arcane
product, but if you can find it, it's delicious and authentic,
unlike almost everything else in this recipe

ZORBA THE SHRIMP

Even though this recipe bears the dread non-Republican icon, its author is Peg Czufin, a.k.a. my Other Mother, and therefore Republican by association, in my opinion, if not hers. Maybe one of these days we will change each other's minds, but for now, at least we agree on dinner.

Suck up to your shrimpmonger like the Liberals do; he will peel and devein the shrimp for you.

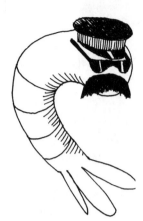

3 tablespoons olive oil, plus more to taste

4 cups chopped onions

2 garlic cloves, chopped, or more to taste

1/2 cup finely chopped parsley

2 tablespoons finely chopped, finger-
  stripped fresh dill

1/2 teaspoon dry mustard

1/2 teaspoon sugar

5 cups canned whole tomatoes, drained and
  chopped (liquid reserved)

2 1/2 cups feta cheese, crumbled

3 pounds large (21 to 30 per pound) shrimp, peeled and
  deveined

Preheat the oven to 425°F.

Heat the olive oil in large saucepan or deep skillet. Add the onions and cook until golden. Add the garlic, parsley, and dill, then stir in the mustard and sugar. Add the tomatoes, 1 cup of the reserved tomato liquid, and about half the feta. Simmer for 30 minutes, adjusting the consistency of the sauce with the remaining tomato liquid; it should not be too thick.

Add the shrimp, cook for 1 minute more, then pour the mixture into a heavy casserole. Sprinkle with the rest of the feta and bake, uncovered, for 10 to 15 minutes, until the shrimp are just done (bright pink, no gray left) and the feta melts.

Serve immediately with rice or orzo and great crunchy bread.

SHRIMP MARGARITA

This is one of those recipes that looks and tastes a whole lot harder than it is. Which makes it equally ideal for special occasions with people you love, and duty dinners for people you don't.

About 1½ pounds large (16 to 20 per pound) shrimp, peeled,
    deveined, and butterflied (split down the back and splatted
    out)
¼ cup fresh lime juice
3 tablespoons unsalted butter
½ cup chopped shallots (or scallions)
⅓ cup tequila
¾ cup heavy cream
1 ripe avocado, sliced
½ bunch of cilantro, coarsely chopped
Salt to taste

Put the shrimp into a resealable plastic bag and pour in the lime juice. Let marinate up to but no longer than 1 hour; otherwise you'll have seviche.

Melt the butter in a wide skillet. Turn the heat to high and, working fast, stir in the shrimp (don't drain) for about 30 seconds, or until the shrimp just begin to turn pink. Add the shallots and sauté for about 1 minute more. Pour in the tequila, cook for 30 seconds more, then, using a slotted spoon, remove the shrimp and set aside. Pour in the cream and add the avocado. Boil for 2 to 3 minutes, or until the sauce starts to thicken (it may take a little longer). Add the cilantro, then return the shrimp to the pan to heat through. Salt to taste, and serve immediately over rice or orzo to sop up that sauce.

REPUBLICAN PORTUGUESE SHRIMP AND LOBSTER STEW

What makes this dish peculiarly Republican is not just its basic peculiarity, but its strong reliance on ketchup, the official vegetable of the GOP. What makes it Portuguese is less clear, but the Republican who gave this recipe to me claims to have received it from somebody who got it from somebody in Lisbon, and since it is so impossibly, preposterously delicious, that's good enough for me.

1 tablespoon olive oil

1¼-pound piece of slab bacon, cut into small cubes

1 large onion, chopped

3 garlic cloves, smashed and chopped

1 tablespoon fragrant dried oregano (Mexican or Greek is best)

½ teaspoon crushed red pepper flakes

1 cup chicken broth

1 cup white wine

⅔ cup ketchup

⅔ cup heavy cream

1¼ pounds large shrimp, shelled and deveined

1¼ pounds cooked lobster meat, cut up

Salt to taste

1 teaspoon Tabasco sauce, or more to taste

Cooked rice or orzo

Chopped parsley, for garnish (optional)

Chopped scallions, for garnish (optional)

Heat the olive oil in a large sauté pan over medium heat. Sauté the bacon in the olive oil until just cooked through, then add the onion, garlic, oregano, and red pepper flakes and sauté, covered, 3 to 4 minutes. Pour in the broth, wine, ketchup, and cream and bring to a boil. Add the shrimp and lobster and cook until the shrimp turn pink and the lobster is heated through, 2 minutes or so. Season with salt and Tabasco and serve over rice or orzo, sprinkled with some chopped parsley and scallion, if you like.

DRUNKEN CRABS

Easy, easy, easy, but $, $, $, so save it for a big impression, like when the first lady's secretary calls and asks if maybe you could host a small dinner for Tony Blair. But he and the missus had better be prepared to forgo their fancy table manners and plunk their elbows on the table, because this dish is one big gorgeous hands-on all-American mess. Provide crab-crackers, little pointy cocktail forks, and

lots of thick napkins (I actually use dish towels). You'll also need a big bowl in the middle of the table to throw the crab shells in.

Your crabmonger is your best friend here; the chopping and slitting are best done by a guy with a big knife and a steady hand.

SERVES 4

1 stick (8 tablespoons) unsalted butter
One 14-ounce can chicken broth
2½ cups dry vermouth
1 bunch of flat-leaf parsley, chopped
6 tablespoons chopped garlic
4 tablespoons soy sauce
4 tablespoons fresh lemon juice
2 teaspoons sugar
4 pounds king crab legs, thawed, chopped into 2- to 3-inch
    sections, shell slit lengthwise, or 4 pounds jumbo shrimp in
    their shells, or a combination of both
1 bunch of scallions, cleaned and chopped
Lemon wedges, for garnish
Tabasco sauce, for passing

Melt the butter in 4- to 6-quart pan or deep skillet. Add the chicken broth, vermouth, ½ cup of the chopped parsley, the garlic, soy sauce, lemon juice, and sugar. Bring to a boil, then lower the heat and simmer for 10 minutes or so. Add the crab and simmer until heated through.

Meanwhile, combine the chopped scallions with the remaining chopped parsley.

Taste the crab mixture and splash in more vermouth (it can only help). Ladle the crab and broth into 4 large shallow bowls, and throw a handful of the scallion-parsley mixture over the top of each. Serve hot with lemon wedges, plenty of Tabasco, and great crusty bread.

NOTE: *This is a perfect dish to serve with Salad in a Glass with May-fair Hotel Dressing (see page 36). Since you've already lost whatever pathetic shreds of dignity you were clinging to, you might as well eat salad with your fingers, too.*

GYPSY ROSE CRAB CAKE

This is stripped-down crab cake at its nakedest and noblest, with nary a cracker crumb, chopped red pepper, or onion in sight. It comes from my friend Cynthia Coldwell in Richmond, Virginia, and you have never had a purer crab cake, unless you are from Baltimore, where I hear the streets are paved with them. Or something like that.

SERVES 4, EXPENSIVELY; BUT REMEMBER, YOU CHOSE TO DO THIS INSTEAD OF BUYING THE LEXUS

1 teaspoon olive oil
1 pound best-quality jumbo lump crabmeat
1 egg, well beaten
4 tablespoons mayonnaise
1 tablespoon whole-grain mustard
1 teaspoon Worcestershire sauce
Dash of Tabasco sauce, plus more for passing
Sea salt and freshly ground black pepper to taste
Lemon wedges, for garnish

Preheat the oven to 425°F.

Brush a baking dish with the olive oil.

Pick over the crabmeat *gently,* as befits anything that costs around $30 a pound, to remove any shell or cartilage, leaving lumps intact (just like Gypsy Rose's). Place in a medium bowl.

In a smaller bowl, thoroughly combine the egg, mayo, mustard, Worcestershire sauce, Tabasco, and salt and pepper. Fold the mixture *gently* into the crabmeat. With a light hand, *gently* form into 4 large cakes and set them into the prepared baking dish. Place in the refrigerator just to set up, 15 to 20 minutes. Check carefully; the crab cakes should be past the gloppy stage they started from, but if they sit too long, they will start to release their liquid and will virtually melt.

Place the baking dish in the oven and bake for 4 minutes, *gently* turning once only, halfway through, when the bottoms are just golden. Turn the oven to broil and, watching closely, cook the second side until just browned, 4 to 5 minutes (or, alternatively sauté over medium-high heat 4 minutes per side). Serve with lemon wedges and more Tabasco, and only to people who would take a bullet for you.

NOTE: *If you like your crab cakes crunchy, dredge the set-up cakes in cornflake crumbs before baking.*

MOM'S MATTAPOISETT MUSSELS

This was originally billed as an appetizer one balmy summer night in Mattapoisett, Massachusetts, a picturesque historic hamlet on Buzzard's Bay. However, as those present were gamely and picturesquely recipe-testing The General's Instant Martini (page 4) with the General himself, they somehow forgot about dinner, and, well, these became It.

3 to 4 pounds mussels, rinsed and debearded if necessary
1 to 2 sticks unsalted butter
Salt and pepper

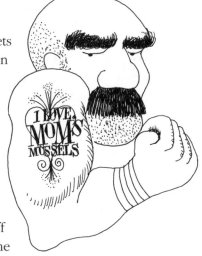

Heat 1 huge or 2 smaller cast-iron skillets over high heat for about 5 minutes (when a drop of gin dances when it hits the skillet, it's ready). Add mussels in 1 layer and cook, shaking the pan, until they start to open, 5 to 10 minutes. The mussel juices will spill out and start crusting, but hang in there, this is a good thing. Add 1 stick of the butter in chunks, and salt and pepper, and, with a wooden spoon, scrape up all the stuff on the bottom and mix. Serve right in the skillets (discarding any unopened mussels), and if you are really going for it, serve the second stick of butter, melted, on the side, to dip the mussels in. This is audience-participation finger food at its messiest and most delicious.

Put the steaks you were going to have for dinner back in the fridge, and invite everybody over for lunch tomorrow. Except the General.

KIT BOND'S DEEP-FRIED HALIBUT CUBES

Halibut, as any Republican knows, is not fish at all, merely fish-shaped seafood. And no one knows that better than Senator Christopher "Kit" Bond, who once landed an eighty-four-pounder on an Alaskan fishing trip with his son Sam. That's a lot of fin, and here's what Kit did with it.

SERVES 6

Preheat the oven to 375°F.

Bake 2 pounds halibut fillets for 12 to 15 minutes or until firm but not flaking. Cut into 2-inch cubes and marinate in ¾ cup vinegar and 1 tablespoon Old Bay seafood seasoning for 10 to 15 minutes. Coat the cubes in a mixture of half mayonnaise and half horseradish cream. Dip the cubes into a mixture of 6 parts cornmeal to 1 part flour, then dip into an egg-and-milk batter (even parts of beaten eggs and skim milk), then back into the cornmeal-flour mixture.

Heat a skillet with canola or other oil to a depth of 3 inches, on medium heat. The oil should be sizzling (test with a drop of water), but not so hot that it boils. Start ladling halibut cubes into the oil, keeping them separate so they don't stick together, and take them out when they turn medium-brown, draining on paper towels as they are done.

Serve the fried halibut cubes hot with more of the horseradish cream, tartar sauce, or cocktail sauce.

BOOLABOOLABAISSE

There is absolutely no evidence to support the notion that everyone who goes to Yale is a Republican, or even a future Republican president. In fact, there is probably considerable evidence to the contrary. But you must admit it's a little easier to picture William Howard Taft or either of the Georges bellowing out the "Bulldog Bow Wow" than, say, Susan Sarandon or Martin Sheen.

Whatever, the recipe comes from a Republican Yalie, so this one's for you, Eli.

½ pound good smokehouse bacon, sliced crosswise into skinny
    little strips
1 tablespoon olive oil
2 big onions, chopped
Grated zest of 1 big orange
2 to 3 canned chipotle peppers, chopped (or 1 tablespoon crushed
    red pepper flakes, but try for the chipotles; it's a smokier taste)
2 teaspoons fennel seeds
Big pinch of saffron
One 28-ounce can tomatoes, crushed
White wine, a little (½ cup) or a lot (½ bottle)
1 pound monkfish cut into cubes (if you can't find it, skip it, or use
    catfish)
3 pounds or so small clams and mussels, mixed
½ pound shrimp
½ pound scallops
1 pound cod or halibut, in big chunks
2 tablespoons minced garlic
1 cup rough-chopped parsley
1 bunch of chopped scallions

Over medium heat, sauté the bacon in the olive oil until almost crisp. Take out the bacon and reserve. Add the onions and cook until soft, 5 minutes, then add the orange zest, chipotles, fennel, and saffron. Cook for a minute or two, then add the tomatoes and turn up the heat. When the mixture boils, reduce the heat and simmer for 10 to 15 minutes until saucey. Add half the wine.

Add the monkfish and raise the heat back to medium-high. When it boils, reduce to medium-low and cook, stirring occasionally, for 10 minutes.

Add the clams and the remaining wine, raise the heat again, and cook for 3 to 4 minutes. Add the mussels. Cover until the shells begin to open.

Add the shrimp, scallops, and cod; stir and cover. Cook for 5 more minutes. If the mixture seems too thick, remember the Republican mantra: *Add more wine.* Stir in the garlic and parsley and reserved bacon (forgot all about the bacon, didn't you?) and serve hot hot hot, garnished with scallions and alongside baskets of hot crusty bread.

NOTE: *Okay, this is a big-deal dish, but it is not only spectacular, it's worth it. So cash in the trust fund. And any leftovers freeze beautifully, she said thriftily.*

CHAPTER FIVE

A CHICKEN IN EVERY POT,

or,

Hoover Should've Stayed in the Kitchen

■ ★

D o you know what Republicans love most about chicken? It tastes just like chicken. Even when it costs $1,000 a plate. But wait: If you act now, you also receive recipes for quail, duck, and rabbit, plus my poignant essay on a Good Old-Fashioned Republican Thanksgiving, including tips on what to do with the leftovers.

FUNERAL CHICKEN

My cousin Joyce, a pious soul and a practical one, explains: "We keep these on hand for funeral dinners. A group of us get together and cook the chickens and get the casseroles ready for the freezer. We make three or four at a time. It's fun and we are always prepared."

SERVES 6 TO 8

¾ cup finely chopped onion
1 cup finely chopped celery
3 sleeves Ritz crackers, crushed
1 whole chicken, poached in
    water, boned and skinned,
    and cut into chunks
½ cup cubed Velveeta cheese
1 can cream of mushroom soup
3 cups broth from cooking the chicken
3 eggs, beaten

Sauté the onion and celery in a little oil or margarine until tender.

Grease a 9 × 13-inch baking dish, and spread 2 sleeves of the crushed crackers on the bottom. Layer over it the chicken, celery, onions, and cheese.

In a medium bowl, mix together the soup, broth, and beaten eggs, and pour the mixture over the casserole. Top with remaining crushed crackers and cover with foil.

At this point either bake at 350°F. for 1 hour, uncovered, or put in the freezer and wait for somebody to die.

EASY-OFF ROAST CHICKEN

Yes, it is easy, but truthfully, it also makes a bit of a mess. But as it also produces perfect, and I mean *perfect* roast chicken, with the crispest skin and the moistest meat—*every time*—it's worth it. And shouldn't you have a self-cleaning oven by now anyway?

SERVES 2 TO 4

> One 3-pound chicken
> 2 lemons, one halved, one left whole and poked full of holes with a
> > fork (work with me here)
> Garlic, as much as you can stand, at least 6 cloves, smashed and
> > coarsely chopped
> Salt and coarsely ground fresh black pepper
> Several sprigs of fresh rosemary, tarragon, oregano, or thyme
> > (optional)
> 1/2 cup chicken broth
> 1/2 cup white wine

Preheat the oven to 500°F., yes 500°.

Rub the chicken inside and out with the halved lemon, garlic, salt, and pepper. Slip some of the whole herbs under the skin, and put the rest inside the cavity along with the punctured lemon. Put the chicken on a rack in a roasting pan, place in the oven, and roast for 1 hour *without ever opening the door,* no matter how nervous you get. You can watch anxiously through the little window if you like, but *do not open the door.*

Remove the lemon from inside the chicken, and pour the juices from the cavity into the pan. Put the chicken on a serving platter and cover with foil for a few minutes while you mash the lemon into the pan juices. Pour in the broth and wine and bring to a simmer, scraping up the browned bits with a wooden spoon. Serve the sauce over the carved bird with some garlic-smashed potatoes.

BIG BONUS:

Instead of roasting the chicken on a rack, cover the bottom of the pan with big chunks of strong wintry vegetables (onions, carrots, potatoes, turnips or parsnips, and one whole head of garlic, cut in half horizontally). Toss them in some good olive oil, sprinkle with coarse salt and pepper, and plop the chicken right on top. Roast as above, finish as above, and guess what you have?

Dinner.

BEER-CAN CHICKEN

Authentic beer-can chicken is a serious item on the good-ole-boy-barbecue-cook-off circuit. As I understand it, a lot of wood chips and a lot of barbecue cooks get marinated in a lot of beer, then the chickens are propped up on the cans and cooked on homemade grills until somebody is declared a winner. My version is similar, though simpler, and does not involve travel to Memphis. The chicken gets just as infused with flavor, arrives just as crispy-brown outside and meltingly moist inside, yet also serves as pregame entertainment for the host and early-arriving guests.

SERVES 3 TO 4

1 can beer

1 big pinch each of cayenne pepper, oregano, garlic salt, pepper, or other potent seasonings of your choice

1 whole chicken, seasoned as for Easy-Off Roast Chicken (page 57), except for the lemon in the cavity, for soon-to-be-obvious reasons

½ to 1 cup white wine

2 tablespoons butter

Preheat the oven to 500°F.

Open the beer and drink half of it. With a church key, poke several additional holes in the top and add the seasonings.

Now, out of respect for the chicken, you can complete the following steps in private, but if your friends have arrived early from the Dow closing down and could use a good laugh (albeit at the chicken's expense), do invite them into the kitchen at this point. Stand the can on a roasting pan and, holding the chicken upright, lower it apologetically over the can until the can fills the main cavity. Gently tug the chicken legs forward to form a little chicken tripod: The chicken should be balanced on the can. I can't explain why this is funny until you see it for yourself, but it is. I don't think it speaks well of my character, or yours, but it is.

Carefully transfer the roasting pan to the oven, close the door, and bake for 1 hour. Do not open the door.

When the chicken is done, *carefully* remove it from the oven, ease it off the can, apologize to it again, and transfer it to a carving platter. Deglaze the roasting pan with what's left in the can, plus some white wine and a little butter. Pour over the chicken and serve.

Okay, now I'm finished, I swear.

GILROY GARLIC FESTIVAL GARLIC CHICKEN AND SAUSAGE

This is so delicious it was selected as a finalist in the 1989 Gilroy Garlic Festival cook-off in Gilroy, California, but since neither I nor my co-cook, my friend Julie Meyer, could pick up and travel to Gilroy (as I had done the previous year; see page 110), we have only the letter to prove it. In this mother of all garlic festivals you can't cook off if you can't cook off in Gilroy, so we are left with naught but a yellowed piece of stationery bearing the logo of the Gilroy Garlic Festival, and our dashed dreams. It's hard not to be bitter.

SERVES 4 TO 6

MARINATE IN A BIG ZIPLOC BAG

1 large onion, sliced
1 green bell pepper, chunked
1 red bell pepper, chunked
1 head of garlic, cloves peeled and left whole, plus 3 more garlic cloves, smashed and chopped
4 whole chicken legs, separated into legs and thighs
2/3 cup Good Seasons Italian dressing (Lite is okay, if you're still in denial)
1/3 cup white wine
Dash of garlic salt
Several dashes of Worcestershire sauce
Several dashes of Tabasco sauce

1 Hillshire Farms Polska Kielbasa (Lite is okay), cut into 1-inch
   pieces

12 small red potatoes, halved if not tiny

½ cup fresh lemon or lime juice (2 to 3 medium lemons or limes),
   plus the rinds

2 heaping tablespoons dried oregano

Lots of freshly ground black pepper

Let both bags marinate in the refrigerator for at least 1 hour, but overnight is even better.

Half an hour before ready to cook, preheat the oven to 400°F. Pour the contents of the chicken-vegetable bag into a rimmed cookie sheet or shallow baking dish and leave uncovered. Put the sausage-potato combo into a second, along with its marinade, and cover tightly with aluminum foil. Place both pans in the oven and bake for 30 minutes. Remove the sausage-potato pan and check to see if the potatoes are done—if not, return, uncovered, to the oven for 5 to 10 minutes. Place the chicken-vegetable pan under the broiler and brown for 15 minutes, turning once. Combine both pans into large gorgeous shallow serving dish, and do a final crisping under the broiler, 5 minutes or so. Pass the sourdough baguettes and prepare for lavish praise: No one has ever not loved this dish. Including, alas, the judges of the Gilroy Garlic Festival. *Sic transit gloria.*

MARY EVELYN (HONEY) GRAYSON'S SWEET AND SMOKY CHICKEN

That's my mom, and yes, Honey is her maiden name. It used to be *MA*honey, but Mom's immigrant great-grandfather, a five-foot-tall leprechaun from County Cork with a long red beard who spoke only Gaelic, changed it so nobody would know he was Irish. None of which has anything to do with this recipe, but make it anyway—it's great.

  1 large onion, sliced
  1 whole chicken, cut up
  3 teaspoons hickory-smoked salt
  1 teaspoon garlic powder
  ½ cup ketchup
  ½ cup pure maple syrup
  ¼ cup vinegar (your favorite—Mom uses Heinz cider vinegar)
  2 tablespoons prepared mustard (that's Gaelic for French's yellow)
  Freshly ground black pepper

Preheat the oven to 350°F.

Place the onion slices in a shallow baking dish and add the chicken pieces in a single layer, skin side up. Sprinkle with the hickory salt and garlic powder.

In a small bowl, combine the ketchup, maple syrup, vinegar, and mustard; grind pepper over. Pour the sauce over the chicken and bake uncovered for 1 hour.

STRAUB'S STICKY CHICKIES IN COKE

There is a small and elegant supermarket in Ladue, Missouri, that is carpeted and lit by crystal chandeliers. It has for generations done business elegantly and discreetly with handwritten house charges, as they assume your house is in the right neighborhood (theirs). At the elegant butcher counter, an elegant silver rack offers index cards entitled "From Straub's Recipe Library." Here is a favorite of mine, in all its elegant entirety.

SERVES 6 TO 8

  ¾ bottle (14-ounce size) catsup (Note "catsup," not "ketchup." Told
      you it was elegant!)
  8 ounces Coca-Cola
  4 whole chicken breasts, skinned, split, and boned

Into a saucepan put the catsup, Coke, and chicken. Do not add flour, salt, or pepper. Cover the pan and bring to a boil, lower the heat, and simmer for 30 minutes. Take the lid off and continue to simmer for another 30 minutes. Turn the chicken several times to prevent sticking and burning.

(My experience: If the sauce is too soupy, take the chicken out after 45 minutes total and keep warm. Crank the heat up and boil the sauce until reduced and thickened, about 15 minutes.)

CHINESE GARLIC CHICKEN

Life is simple if you are a Republican: Anything with soy sauce is Chinese; anything with garlic is better; anything with hot red pepper wins. And, in this case, an hour later, you'll want it again.

SERVES 4

3 tablespoons vegetable oil
3½-pound frying chicken, cut into serving pieces
1 whole head of garlic, peeled, smashed, and coarsely chopped
2 small dried hot red chile peppers, or 2 teaspoons crushed red
    pepper flakes
¾ cup white vinegar
¼ cup soy sauce
2 tablespoons honey
1 tablespoon sesame seeds, toasted in a dry skillet (careful!)
½ cup chopped scallions, for garnish
½ cup chopped fresh parsley or cilantro, for garnish
Cooked rice

Heat the oil in a large, heavy skillet and brown the chicken well. Add the garlic and peppers toward the end. Add the vinegar, soy sauce, and honey and cook over medium-high heat until the chicken is done, 10 to 15 minutes. The white meat will probably be done earlier, so pull those pieces out and wait until the dark-meat pieces are done.

Add some water (or white wine or chicken broth) to the pan,

scraping up the browned bits, and pour the sauce over the chicken. Sprinkle the chicken with the toasted sesame seeds, scallions, and parsley and serve with rice. At least once a week.

SPICY GARLIC POLLO AND PATATAS IN A POT

By now the alert reader will have noticed a certain reliance in this book on garlic. So be it. All I can tell you is I have never seen a Republican vampire.

SERVES 4

> 1 large chicken, cut into 8 pieces
> 12 garlic cloves, crushed
> 1 tablespoon plus 2 teaspoons coarse salt
> 1 tablespoon coarsely ground black pepper
> 2 tablespoons vegetable oil
> ¾ cup red wine vinegar
> 2 tablespoons good olive oil (optional)
> 4 bay leaves
> 2 tablespoons dried thyme
> 2 tablespoons dried marjoram
> 2 chopped hot chiles (serranos, jalapeños, whatever), or canned
>   chipotle peppers
> Garlic Patatas (recipe follows)

Rub the chicken with the garlic, 1 tablespoon of the salt, and the pepper. Refrigerate for 2 to 3 hours, and make the patatas sometime in there.

Heat the vegetable oil in a large skillet and brown the chicken. Put the chicken in a large pot. Add the vinegar to the skillet and bring to a boil, scraping up the good crusty bits. Pour it all over the chicken in the pot. Add the olive oil, if using, the remaining 2 teaspoons salt, the bay leaves, thyme, and marjoram; bring to a boil, then cover and simmer. Every few minutes, uncover and stir. After about 30 minutes, uncover, taste, adjust the seasonings if necessary, and add the chiles.

Cook for 10 minutes more, then add the Garlic Patatas and heat through, 5 minutes or so.

GARLIC PATATAS

You say potato, I say patata, but as long as we both say garlic, we are speaking the same language.

2 pounds tiny new potatoes
1/2 cup unsalted butter
1 tablespoon oil
12 garlic cloves, sliced or minced
1 tablespoon salt
Freshly ground black pepper to taste
1 1/2 tablespoons fresh lemon or lime juice
1/2 teaspoon Tabasco sauce, or more to
    taste

Boil the potatoes in salted water until tender but not mooshy, 20 minutes or so, then drain and put aside.

Heat the butter and oil in a large saucepan. Add the potatoes and sauté for 10 minutes, or until the skins get a bit crispy. Add the garlic, salt, pepper, lemon juice, and Tabasco and cook for 3 to 4 minutes, or until the garlic turns golden brown, just short of burning.

This is a great side dish for anything, by the way, and makes a terrific appetizer as well. Just spear with toothpicks and stand back.

NOTE: *If you eat this dish right away, instead of sensibly refrigerating it until the fat hardens so you can lift it off before reheating and serving, you won't notice the fat at all, particularly if you had your eyes modestly averted while not draining the browned chicken and then boldly adding the optional olive oil. It's fabulous either way.*

BUFFALO RIGHT WINGS

(An Homage to Pat Buchanan)

SERVES 4 TO 6

>   3 pounds chicken wings, cut into 3 pieces (yes, use the little pointy
>   ends too)
>   10 garlic cloves, coarsely chopped
>   2 teaspoons crushed red pepper flakes
>   Coarse salt to taste
>   Coarsely ground black pepper to taste
>
>   Celery sticks, for dipping
>   Blue cheese dressing, for dipping

Put the chicken wings, garlic, and seasonings into a bowl and mix well with your hands. Let marinate for 1 hour (or overnight in the fridge, covered tightly, but I still wouldn't stick it next to the milk).

Preheat the oven to 450°F.

Spread the chicken wings out in a baking pan and bake uncovered for about 1 hour. Check after 45 minutes, but these are supposed to be almost-black-crispy, particularly the wing tips, which you should be able to eat bones and all.

Serve with this sauce:

>   2 tablespoons butter
>   One-half 12-ounce bottle Frank's Original Red Hot Cayenne Pepper
>   Sauce

Melt the butter into the hot sauce in a small pan over low heat. Taste; if it's too hot for you, you weenie, add more butter. Pour over the wings, toss, and serve.

Serve with celery sticks and bottled blue cheese dressing to dip in (add extra crumbled blue cheese if you like).

DR. CURRAN'S THIGHS

Dr. Curran—ah, let's just call him Smith, not his real name, of course—is a Republican plastic surgeon in Seattle, a town that, if you look at a relief map of the United States, could easily topple into Puget Sound, it leans that far left. So in the interest of not jeopardizing his extremely prosperous practice, and as part of our Plastic Surgeon Protection Program, we will merely comment that while Dr. C. does a lively business making faces tighter, bosoms bigger, and bottoms smaller, these thighs are perfect just as they are.

SERVES 4 TO 6

    8 chicken thighs, skin on
    4 tablespoons dark Asian sesame oil
    2 teaspoons bottled liquid smoke
    3 tablespoons lemon pepper, plus more to sprinkle over later

Place the chicken thighs in a large bowl and douse with the sesame oil and liquid smoke. Sprinkle very generously with the lemon pepper and toss well by hand; then, Dr. Curran reminds us, thoroughly wash your hands, then wash your hands again, of the whole thing, in Whitewater fashion.

Prepare a charcoal or gas grill. Cook the chicken slowly over low heat, turning every 20 to 30 minutes, until crispy but still moist, about 1¼ hours total. Serve with more lemon pepper to sprinkle over.

LINDA PEARCE'S GRILLED DAN QUAYLE

Linda Pearce is *the* antiques dealer in Kansas City, and if you think that an oxymoron, I can assure you her client list is full of "Page Six" names from New York to Paris to London to Buenos Aires, many familiar from certain administrations—and regimes—best not mentioned here. Superb and world-class as her merchandise is, I am certain much of her success is due to the entertainment derived from simply talking to her, as her whiskey-'n'-Winstons voice makes Harvey Fierstein sound like Megan Mullally. Linda says (in that voice) the only difficult thing about this dish is finding the quayle; you need a Republican for that. But luckily, in Kansas City, finding a Republican is not that hard.

Linda serves this with creamed hominy and a spinach salad with red onion, avocado, and orange. Creamed hominy? Wait here; I think I have to call her back.

SERVES 4

    8 quail
    1 cup chicken bouillon
    1 teaspoon seasoned salt
    1 tablespoon instant minced onion
    1/8 teaspoon garlic powder
    1 tablespoon lemon juice
    1/4 cup soy sauce
    1/4 cup sherry
    8 tablespoons honey
    8 bacon slices

Place the quail in a large resealable plastic bag and add the bouillon, seasoned salt, onion, garlic powder, lemon juice, soy sauce, sherry, and honey. Marinate for 6 to 24 hours.

Prepare a charcoal or gas grill.

Remove the quail from the marinade and wrap each in a bacon slice. Grill for 20 minutes, turning every 5 minutes, or until the birds are golden and the bacon is crisp.

FAVORITE WILD DUCK OF THE NRA WITH SOOZY'S BOOZY SAUSAGE WILD RICE WITH CHERRIES

This dish is as rich as a Republican after a tax cut, but it's worth it. I cavalierly call for three roasted wild ducks, on the chance that you happen to have a duck hunter in the family, but if you don't, domestic duck will do, or even three pounds or so of cooked chicken thighs or leftover turkey (dark meat is best).

2 sticks (1 cup) unsalted butter

½ cup Dijon mustard

2 tablespoons Worcestershire sauce

1 cup fresh lemon juice (about 4 to 6 lemons)

4 cloves garlic, smashed and chopped

Salt and freshly ground black pepper to taste

Tabasco sauce to taste

3 wild ducks, or domestic, cooked the way the cookbook your mother gave you when you got married says to, or 3 pounds cooked chicken or turkey thighs

2 bunches of scallions, chopped

Soozy's Boozy Sausage Wild Rice with Cherries (recipe follows)

Chopped fresh parsley, for garnish

Preheat the oven to 325°F.

In a medium saucepan, melt the butter. Stir in the mustard, Worcestershire sauce, lemon juice, garlic, salt, and pepper. Adjust to taste, and add the Tabasco.

Shred or cut the duck meat into skinny pieces and toss with the butter mixture and ¾ of the scallions (reserving the rest for garnish). Place in a casserole and bake until just hot, no more than 30 minutes. You don't want to dry out the meat. Keep warm while you prepare the rice.

Serve the rice alongside the duck and shower parsley and the remaining scallions over all.

SOOZY'S BOOZY SAUSAGE WILD RICE WITH CHERRIES

SERVES 6

1 to 2 tablespoons oil

½ pound sweet Italian sausage, taken out of casing and
    crumbled

1 big onion, chopped

2 tablespoons butter

One 6-ounce box Uncle Ben's Long Grain and Wild Rice

2 cups water

One 16-ounce can pitted black cherries, packed in heavy syrup,
    drained and soaked in bourbon or brandy to cover for at
    least 1 hour

In 1 tablespoon of the oil, sauté the sausage until no longer pink; remove and reserve. Add the onion (and more oil if necessary) and sauté until tender. Add the butter, and sauté the rice until nice and toasty. Add the rice's seasoning packet and the water, bring to a boil, then reduce the heat to a simmer. Cover and cook until the liquid is absorbed and the rice is done. Add the reserved sausage and the now-soused black cherries, including some of the very potent liquid, if desired (I always desire).

THUMPER EST MORT

Yes, I know, but rabbit tastes like chicken, and it's something else you can kill.

SERVES 4

- 6 strips good gutsy smoky bacon
- 2 tablespoons olive oil
- 1 tablespoon butter
- 3 pounds rabbit, cut up, seasoned with garlic salt and lots of fresh pepper
- 1 big onion, sliced
- 1 to 2 tablespoons smashed and coarsely chopped garlic
- 1 bay leaf
- 4 sprigs of fresh rosemary, or 2 teaspoons dried rosemary
- 4 tablespoons chopped Italian parsley, plus more for garnish
- 1 cup chicken stock
- 2 cups red wine
- 4 big roasted red peppers, torn into slices (good bottled ones work just fine)
- Chopped scallions, for garnish

In a flame-loving casserole (such as Le Creuset), cook the bacon in the olive oil and butter for about 3 minutes. Add the rabbit and brown all over until crispy. Remove the bacon and rabbit and set them aside on a platter to allow the juices to collect.

In the reserved fat, brown the onion and garlic, then return the rabbit and bacon and the meat juices to the pot. Add the bay leaf, rosemary, and parsley, and deglaze with the chicken stock and wine. Bring to a boil and simmer, covered, for 45 minutes, or until tender.

Add the roasted red peppers to the casserole and simmer, stirring, for 15 minutes.

FINAL TOUCH

¼ cup olive oil
1 tablespoon chopped garlic
4 drained anchovy fillets, coarsely chopped
½ cup red vinegar

In a small skillet, heat the olive oil. Sauté the garlic in the olive oil until soft, then add the anchovies and cook until they are more or less dissolved. Add the vinegar and reduce a bit. Stir the mixture into the casserole and serve hot, garnished if you like with more parsley and chopped scallions.

NOTE: *This is incredible served with garlic-horseradish-mashed-potatoes-and-turnips made with buttermilk and butter. But then, what isn't?*

GOOD OLD-FASHIONED REPUBLICAN THANKSGIVING FRIDAY NIGHT LEFTOVER SURPRISE

Republicans love a good old-fashioned Thanksgiving, especially those commencing with Good Old-Fashioned Republican Old-Fashioneds (page 6).

As a matter of fact, if Norman Rockwell was not a Republican, there is no doubt he certainly knew a few. How else could he have painted that *Saturday Evening Post* cover? Of course, he left a couple hours too soon. Before the party really kicked in, before Grandpa got drunk and started singing "Lucille." Before Cousin Bob got drunk and wound up facedown in the giblet gravy. Before Nana got drunk and served the pecan pie raw. Before Aunt Susie (that's me) got drunk and announced she was pro-choice. Which, as nearly as I can recall, is what really started the fistfight; not, as it was later alleged, the rumor we had run out of Jack Daniel's, Absolut, Beefeater, and Jose Cuervo, and might have to resort to rum.

At any rate, it is every Republican's favorite holiday, and mainly because of all the wonderful things you can do with the leftovers.

Reheat the turkey.
Reheat the stuffing.
Reheat the mashed potatoes.
Reheat the giblet gravy.
Reheat the spinach casserole.
Reheat the scalloped oysters nobody touched yesterday anyway.
Reheat the Brussels sprouts   "   "   "   "
*Get the cranberry relish and Aunt Shari's Green Stuff out of the
    fridge.*
Cook the pecan pie.
And that's it. Simple, fun, creative, and everybody loves it.

CHAPTER SIX

JOHN WAYNE ATE HERE:
Manly Main Dishes,
Mainly Starring Meat

M en Who Eat Meat, and the Women Who Love Them, and other accurate descriptions of the Republican party. This chapter is a hearty one, including such red-blooded dishes as Mike's Single-Malt Spareribs, Evelyn's Pickle-Stuffed Clay Pot Flank Steak, Magic Never-Fail Christmas Day Roast Beef, the Fremont, Ohio, Fire Department's Censored Sausage and Stuffing Stew, four great meat loaf recipes, and five, *five,* for chili.

Chili, of course, is a real Republican favorite as it is perfect for when the guys gather around the TV to watch Republican Sporting Events (Republican Sporting Events include The Masters, The Open, The British Open, The PGA, the Army-Navy game, Harvard *v.* Yale and Roe *v.* Wade).

MAGIC NEVER-FAIL CHRISTMAS DAY ROAST BEEF

This is one of those card-trick recipes that works every time, producing perfect roast beef: crisp brown end cuts, rosy medium meat, and also blue rare meat—something for everyone, no matter the size of the roast. The secret is in not opening the oven door. In my family, we seal the door with masking tape, with grim warnings in rude language written in red Sharpies. This recipe is bulletproof.

For twelve people, figure six ribs; that's about a fifteen-pound roast.

> One 3- to 18-pound rolled rib or standing rib roast (Size Doesn't
> Matter) at room temperature
> Many, many garlic cloves, sliced thin (for a 6-rib roast, at least
> 1 whole head of garlic)
> Salt and freshly ground black pepper
> Horseradish sour cream, for serving

Preheat the oven to 375°F.

With a sharp knife, cut little slits all over the fat and meat of the roast and insert garlic slices. Rub generously with salt and pepper.

Place the roast, fat side up, in a shallow roasting pan and roast for exactly 1 hour. Turn off the heat, but do not open the oven door. No matter how long it is until dinner, *DO NOT OPEN THE OVEN DOOR;* let the roast just sit in there and sulk.

About 45 minutes before serving time, turn the oven on again to 375°F., still without opening the door.

After 30 minutes, take the roast out and let it rest in a warm place, loosely tented with foil, for 10 to 15 minutes, then serve with the pan juices and horseradish sour cream.

THE FORBES FAMILY'S FAVORITE EASY BEEF STEW

Ever wonder what people like the Rockefellers or the Fords or the Gateses or the Whitneys or the Windsors or the Winfrey eat for supper? Betcha not this. And whatever it is, betcha it's not half as good or easy as what Sabina Forbes whips up for Steve and their four daughters whenever the mood strikes, which, as it happens, is often. It's good to be the Republican.

SERVES 6

2 pounds beef stew meat
1 tablespoon flour
2 tablespoons olive oil
1 can Campbell's beef consommé
1 pound carrots, scraped and cut up
6 leeks, trimmed, split, and soaked to remove grit
6 medium-size red potatoes, peeled (or not; I like them with the skins)
6 ounces ketchup

Cut the beef into cubes. In a bowl, sprinkle the flour on the beef and mix.

In a big pot, warm the olive oil and add the beef. Sauté for 2 minutes. Pour in the beef consommé and stir, making sure the flour does not stick to the bottom of the pan. Add the carrots, leeks, and potatoes. Bring everything to a boil. Once the stew is boiling, put on very low heat and cover. Cook for 1½ hours; add the ketchup and stir. Cook for another hour, but be careful not to let the stew burn at the bottom of the pot. Check it often.

Serve warm with hot buttered fresh bread.

EVELYN'S PICKLE-STUFFED CLAY POT FLANK STEAK

This recipe presumes you bought one of those Romertopf clay-pot ovens back in the 1970s, probably right around the time you got that Rival Crockpot for a wedding present. The concept, in case you don't know, is that the food cooks on its own, in an ancient clay-pot manner, manufacturing amazingly juicy juices with little or no fat, and with no help from you. I am not kidding about this, and I hate getting tough with you, but if you don't have a Romertopf clay pot, go on eBay this instant and have one overnighted; this recipe is that good.

Tenderizing the meat is a very important step, and you must persevere. If your butcher is stubborn, find another butcher, or get one of those mallet things with the points and pound it to death yourself. Curiously refreshing exercise, by the way.

SERVES 6 TO 8

Two 1½-pound flank steaks, run through your butcher's tenderizer
    twice
Salt and freshly ground black pepper
2 tablespoons dried marjoram
1 cup Dijon or brown mustard, or enough to coat the meat well
2 large dill pickles, sliced long and broad and thin
1 pound Muenster cheese, sliced thin
Big chunks of vegetables: onions, turnips, carrots, potatoes,
    zucchini, Brussels sprouts, even wedges of cabbage—your
    choice

Do not preheat the oven. Soak both halves of a clay pot in water to cover for 15 minutes.

Meanwhile, season one side of the steaks with salt, pepper, and marjoram. Then spread each with mustard, put down a layer of pickle slices (crosswise of the meat), then layer the cheese slices. Roll each steak into a log and tie with string. Place the rolled steaks in the bottom of the pot. Cover and stick into a cold oven and turn it to 425°F. Bake for 40 minutes. Remove the lid, surround the meat with the vegetables, then cover again and bake for 40 minutes more.

To serve, lift the meat out and place it on a deep platter. Cut the strings and slice the meat. Ladle the vegetables and juices over all, saving excess vegetables, etc., in the pot for certain seconds.

This is wildly delicious, and the juices are incredible. Have a lot of something starchy (onion sourdough bread or rice, or even better, barley) to soak them up.

BARLEY BONUS:

This is a wonderful and unusual side dish for anything beef: Toast medium pearl barley in butter in a saucepan, then follow package instructions to cook, substituting beef broth for water. Stir in chopped scallions. A little kid I know calls it "soggy popcorn," and dotes on it.

LETTY GOCHBERG'S BARBECUED POT ROAST

Technically, Letty Gochberg is too young to be a living legend, but I defy you to find any Republican in New York who would dispute it. Of course, I pretty much defy you to find any Republican in New York, period, but we have discussed that. Anyway, one of the many reasons Letty is so famous is that she is one fabulous family cook. And when Letty is cooking, her family includes anybody who hears Letty is cooking, like the time her daughter called and asked if she could bring some friends from school for the Jewish holidays and forty-four kids showed up.

Letty also cooks for her own fund-raisers. I don't recall ever hearing that said about Pamela Harriman or Katharine Graham.

SERVES 8

4 pounds round roast, trimmed
2 pounds onions, sliced
16 ounces barbecue sauce, your favorite bottled brand or Keith's
    Bourbon and Butter Barbecue Sauce (recipe follows)

Preheat the oven to 350°F.

Place the roast on 2 layers of heavy-duty aluminum foil placed in a roasting pan (long pieces). Cover the meat with the onions and pour the barbecue sauce over. Seal the foil tightly and roast for 2½ hours minimum; open and pierce the meat with a fork. If it's not falling apart, it's not done, so reseal and cook for 30 minutes more.

KEITH'S BOURBON AND BUTTER BARBECUE SAUCE

Keith Beshears was my godfather, a brilliant, handsome, talented man who in 1955 owned the first and, as it ultimately turned out, only powder-blue T-Bird in Springfield, Missouri, and who dearly, dearly, dearly loved butter. And bourbon. I was riding back to St. Louis with him one New Year's Day many years ago, each of us silently suffering the morning-afters of our respective night-befores, when we drove through Bourbon, Missouri. You always know when you are in Bourbon because of the town's huge elevated water tower spelling out BOURBON in fifteen-foot-high letters. Keith, who had not spoken in 125 miles, and would not again for the next 75, sighed: "If I thought they meant that, I'd move here."

MAKES A COUPLE OF FIFTHS

1 large onion, chopped
1 heaping tablespoon chopped garlic, or more to taste
1½ sticks (¾ cup) butter, melted
3 cups ketchup
¼ cup molasses
1½ cups bourbon
½ cup white vinegar
Tabasco sauce to taste

In a large saucepan, cook the onion and garlic in the butter, then stir in all else except the Tabasco. Bring to a boil, then lower the heat and simmer. Theoretically, this will cook out the alcohol, leaving only the flavor, but have you ever really believed that? Anyway, taste for seasoning—it may need more bourbon. Add Tabasco.

HELEN'S REPUBLICAN SHEPHERD'S PIE

You probably didn't think shepherd's pie was Republican because, try as you might, you can't think of any Republican shepherds. I myself am trying to picture George Bush with a crook, leading fluffy white animals going baa-a-a-a. Now wait; maybe it's not really that hard. Anyway, this shepherd's pie comes from Helen Haughey, the New Zealand–born mother of Rachel Oliver, who is the wife of Jack Oliver, former deputy chairman of the RNC. There. Now it's Republican. Or at least fusion—and unusually delicious.

1½ pounds ground lamb (or beef)
½ onion, chopped
3 tablespoons Major Grey's chutney
3 tablespoons soy sauce
¼ cup canned tomato sauce
Salt and freshly ground black pepper
4 large potatoes, mashed and
    prepared your favorite way
    (Helen leaves them plain)
Paprika, to sprinkle over

Preheat the oven to 350°F.

Brown the lamb and onion, then add the chutney, soy sauce, and tomato sauce. Season to taste with salt and pepper and simmer for 15 minutes.

Place the meat mixture in a casserole dish and spread the mashed potatoes on top, scoring with a fork. Sprinkle with paprika and bake for 30 minutes, or until the top is lightly browned.

IRENE HALLIGAN'S MIGHTY MAC AND CHEESE

This is one of those Sunday-night Fire Island "Oh, shoot, we missed the last ferry" dishes Irene is semi-ashamed to own up to, but it is pure womb food, comforting and indecently delicious. Plus, she has that Sutton Place recipe on page 27 to redeem her reputation.

SERVES 6 TO 8

1½ pounds lean ground beef
1 tablespoon oil
½ pound elbow macaroni, cooked until just al dente (read: bite-y,
    not mooshy)
2 cans Campbell's condensed cream of tomato soup, undiluted
¼ pound sharp cheese, diced
Salt and pepper

Sauté the beef rapidly in the oil, breaking it up. Add the al dente macaroni and the soup and mix well over low heat. Stir in the cheese and seasonings and simmer for 10 minutes, or until the cheese is melted and all is combined.

LETTY'S METROPOLITAN MEAT LOAF

I believe I neglected to mention that Letty Gochberg (see page 78) once trained at the Metropolitan Opera, and this is another of the specialties that make her friends sing.

SERVES 8 TO 10

> 3 pounds ground round
> 2 eggs
> Two 1-ounce packages Lipton Onion Soup Mix
> 1 cup ketchup, divided
> 1 large onion, sliced
> Red wine or sherry, for deglazing the pan
> One 10½-ounce can prepared onion gravy

Preheat the oven to 350°F.

In a large bowl, gently mix the meat, eggs, soup mix, and ½ cup of the ketchup, making sure the eggs are well incorporated. Shape into a meat loaf in a baking pan, and distribute the sliced onions over, pressing them into the meat loaf slightly.

Bake uncovered for 45 minutes. Remove from the oven and spread the remaining ½ cup ketchup over the onions to top off the meat loaf. Return to the oven and bake for another 15 minutes, or until the juices run clear. The surface should be well browned and the onions caramelized. Serve with mashed potatoes and this gravy:

Remove the meat loaf from the pan and place on a platter. Drain the fat from the meat-loaf pan, and deglaze the pan over medium heat with red wine or sherry. Stir in the onion gravy, and season to taste.

Serve the meat loaf and gravy with mashed potatoes.

BACON CHEESEBURGER MEAT LOAF

Another of those spiritual Republican recipes: If you find a peaceful place to meditate, sit in the Lotus position, take long, deep breaths, intone *ohhmmmmms,* and listen carefully, you can actually hear your arteries slapping shut.

SERVES 6 TO 8

MEAT LOAF

2 pounds ground beef
1½ cups cubed cheese (Swiss, Cheddar, Monterey Jack, or any
    combination)
2 eggs, beaten
½ cup chopped onion
½ cup chopped green bell pepper
1 teaspoon garlic salt, or to taste
Freshly ground black pepper to taste
1 teaspoon celery salt
½ teaspoon paprika
2½ cups milk
1 cup dry bread crumbs
8 slices good smoky bacon

SAUCE

One 8-ounce can tomato sauce
5 tablespoons mustard, whatever kind
    you like best on cheeseburgers
2 tablespoons white sugar
2 tablespoons brown sugar
2 tablespoons vinegar

Preheat the oven to 350°F.

In a large bowl, gently mix all the meat-loaf ingredients except the bacon together. Shape the meat loaf and put into a greased loaf pan. Drape the bacon over the loaf to cover. Use more if necessary to cover the top.

Mix the sauce and pour over the meat loaf. Bake uncovered, basting occasionally, for 1½ hours, or until the juices run clear and the bacon is crisp.

MOTHER'S COMPANY HAM LOAF

This is ridiculously rewarding. My mother's recipe says it serves eight, and I will only add, they'd better be teamsters and they'd better be hungry. But since nobody ever has just one helping, that's probably accurate enough.

SERVES 8 TO 10

HAM LOAF

2 pounds ground ham
1 pound ground lean pork
1½ cups cracker crumbs (Saltines or Ritz; welcome to the G.O.P.)
½ cup chopped onion
4 eggs, beaten
1¼ teaspoons salt
Freshly ground black pepper to taste
2 cups milk
Chopped parsley

SAUCE

1 cup brown sugar
1½ teaspoons dry mustard
½ cup vinegar

In a large bowl, combine all the meat-loaf ingredients except the parsley and mix well. Shape the mixture into 2 loaves and place in greased loaf pans. (You can freeze at this point, à la Funeral Chicken, page 57.)

Preheat the oven to 350°F.

Cook the ingredients for the sauce over low heat until the sugar and mustard are dissolved. Pour the sauce over the loaves and bake for 1 hour and 45 minutes.

Turn the loaves out onto a serving platter and pour the indescribable juices over. Garnish with the parsley. Die, then go to heaven.

MARY HAD SOME LITTLE LAMB LOAVES

Little kids just love these, but then, so do emotionally secure adults. The yogurt sauce is terrific spooned over them, but you can also serve mint jelly and pretend it's for the children.

MAKES 12 LITTLE LOAVES (6 SERVINGS)

YOGURT SAUCE

One 8-ounce carton plain yogurt
2 tablespoons chopped fresh mint
1 minced scallion
1 garlic clove, minced
Pinch of ground cumin
Garlic salt to taste
Small pinch of crushed red pepper flakes
Juice of ½ lemon

LAMB LOAVES

3 garlic cloves, smashed and minced, sautéed briefly in a little oil
1 pound lean ground lamb
½ pound lean ground beef
2 cups soft bread crumbs
1 can Campbell's condensed onion soup, undiluted
½ teaspoon dried oregano
Salt and freshly ground black pepper to taste
Pine nuts
Mint leaves for garnish, optional

Mix all the yogurt-sauce ingredients together in a bowl. Set aside for at least 30 minutes, then adjust the seasonings to taste. It should pack some punch.

Meanwhile, preheat the oven to 400°F.

In a large bowl, mix all the lamb-loaf ingredients except the pine nuts and the mint leaves until just blended. Don't overmix. Spoon the meat mixture into 12 ungreased nonstick 2½-inch muffin cups, pressing in gently. Sprinkle the pine nuts over the tops, about 12 per little loaf. Bake uncovered for 15 minutes, or until the meat and nuts brown and the meat is no longer pink inside (but don't overcook).

Garnish with a few mint leaves, if using, and serve with the yogurt sauce.

TEXICAN STEW

This is a preview of coming attractions, a kind of segue from beef into chili. This has chunks of meat and cornlike bits, but it's a form of chili all right, and one that kids will gobble up. Serve jalapeño slices alongside for the grown-ups. And did I—or need I—mention Tabasco?

Only a Republican could say Mexicorn with a straight face.

SERVES 4 TO 6

2 pounds stew meat (cubed chuck works fine)
2 tablespoons vegetable or olive oil
2 large onions, chopped
4 green bell peppers, chopped
5 big garlic cloves, smashed and chopped
Salt and pepper to taste
2 to 3 big tablespoons chili powder
Two 1-pound cans tomatoes, undrained
2 cans kidney beans, drained
3 cans Mexicorn, drained

In a big skillet, brown the meat in the oil. Pour out the excess fat, then add the onions, peppers, garlic, and salt and pepper. Add the chili powder and cook for 2 minutes. Add the tomatoes, simmer 1 hour, then add the beans and simmer 1 hour more. Stir in the Mexicorn just to heat through, taste for seasoning, and serve.

SENATOR DANFORTH'S CHILI

Jack Danforth is a big and big-hearted man. Not only generous with his recipes, he is also exceptionally giving of his time and patience. When my son Tim was nine years old, he and I visited with the senator in Washington. This was the thank-you letter Tim wrote.

3/29/1984

Dear Jack,

I am glad you could take time out of your busy life to see us. It was a sparkling thrill to meet you. I found the ups and downs of being a senator, ups, the publicity, downs the work and the trouble. Anyway, I enjoyed learning about you and your life. Thanks!

> *Your friend,*
> *Timmy [Dick Grayson's grandson]*

SERVES 10 TO 12

3½ pounds top round, cut in ½-inch cubes
5 tablespoons oil
2 cups onion, coarsely chopped
4 garlic cloves, minced
4 tablespoons chili powder
1½ teaspoons oregano
1½ teaspoons ground cumin
1 teaspoon crushed red pepper flakes
2 cups beef broth
One 1-pound 3-ounce can whole tomatoes
One 6-ounce can tomato paste
1 tablespoon salt
1 teaspoon sugar
3 cans kidney or chili beans
1 to 2 tablespoons yellow cornmeal

Pat the meat dry with paper towels. Heat 3 tablespoons of the oil in a large, heavy pot. When hot, add the meat all at once. Sear until all the pieces are lightly browned, 3 to 4 minutes. Use a spoon and turn the meat constantly.

Transfer the meat to a bowl and add the remaining 2 tablespoons oil to the pot. Add the onion and garlic and sauté until the onion is wilted but not browned. Stir in the chili powder, oregano, cumin, and red pepper flakes; mix well until the onions are coated. Add the beef broth, tomatoes (juice and all), tomato paste, salt, and sugar, mixing well. Break up the tomatoes with the back of a spoon. Pour out a portion of juice from the meat bowl and return the meat to the pot; cover and simmer for 1 hour. Uncover and simmer for 40 to 50 minutes, then add the beans. Cool, cover, and refrigerate overnight.

To serve, bring slowly to a boil and simmer until heated through. Thicken with cornmeal to the desired consistency.

NOTE: *If you can't find a 1-pound 3-ounce can of tomatoes—I couldn't—use the typical fat can (1 pound 12 ounces) but not the juice. Or be true to the senator and just save the leftover 9 ounces of tomatoes and juice and make a teensy weensy marinara sauce or something.*

SENATOR GOLDWATER'S CHILI

The original secret chili spice mix was the personal creation of the beloved (and not just by Republicans) Arizona senator Barry Goldwater. His chili beat a Texas senator's in a famous chili duel in Washington, D.C., back in the 1970s.

The senator's famous chili mix can be purchased at Goldwater's Foods of Arizona, P.O. Box 9846, Scottsdale, AZ 85252, or at www.goldwaters.net. Or just go to Arizona and stop into any food store; I think it is against the law there not to stock it. I take boxes of these as hostess gifts and always get invited back.

SERVES 6

> 2 pounds lean ground beef (or ground turkey, or cubed lean pork)
> One 15-ounce can tomato sauce
> 1 can beer or water
> One 2.5-ounce package Senator Goldwater's Chili Mix
> 1 can each pinto, kidney, and black beans, drained and rinsed

Brown the beef in a 2- to 3-quart pot and drain the fat. Add the tomato sauce and beer (or water) and stir in the Chili Mix packet. Simmer for 30 minutes. Now add the beans and simmer for another 30 minutes "to get the flavors acquainted." Serve with corn bread and some chopped jalapeños to stir in.

POLLY BERGEN'S CHILI

Proving yet again that in New York you can round up twenty-five Democrats at the drop of an ERA meeting, whereas it would take a decree from Sir Rudy Giuliani to get that many Republicans together in this town, and most of them would have to commute from Connecticut.

As I am quite possibly the only Republican Polly Bergen knows, I am particularly grateful to her for this terrific crowd-pleasing recipe, but then Polly is used to pleasing crowds, isn't she? Not only is she an amazing singer and actress, she is also a famous cook, although up until now, only among Liberals. Polly, we're gonna make you a star.

SERVES 25

3 garlic cloves, minced
Olive oil
6 large onions, finely chopped
6 large green bell peppers, finely chopped
6 pounds ground round or chuck (fatter but tastier)
Five 1-pound cans Italian-style tomatoes
Four to six 1-pound cans drained dark kidney beans
Two 6-ounce cans tomato paste
Salt and pepper to taste
2 teaspoons wine vinegar
5 whole cloves
3 bay leaves
4 tablespoons chili powder, or more to taste
Sugar to taste
2 teaspoons cumin

In a large roaster, sauté the garlic in olive oil and remove. Sauté the onions and peppers until golden, remove, and drain. Add the meat to the olive oil, separate with a fork, and cook until the meat is no longer red—okay, it will be gray, and we both know it—in color. Drain off the fat.

Add the onions and peppers to the meat, mix well, then add all the remaining ingredients. Cover and simmer over low heat for 1 hour. Simmer uncovered for another hour. Remove the cloves and bay leaves before serving.

SANDY BERKELEY'S WHITE BEAN CHILI

If there is a Guinness Book of World Mayors, Kansas City's Dick Berkeley holds all the records. Not only was he elected to the office for three consecutive terms (that is not only a record, I'm not at all sure it's even legal), he was mayor pro tem for eight years before that. Doing the math, that makes Dick Berkeley mayor of Kansas City, Missouri, for twenty years. Twenty years! What were you doing between 1971 and 1991? Among a few thousand other things, Sandy (Mrs.) Berkeley was making chili, and the world is a better place for it.

SERVES 6 TO 8

1 pound large white beans, soaked overnight in water and drained
6 cups chicken broth
2 garlic cloves, minced
2 medium onions, chopped and divided
1 tablespoon oil
Two 4-ounce cans chopped green chiles
2 teaspoons ground cumin
1½ teaspoons dried oregano
¼ teaspoon ground cloves
¼ teaspoon cayenne pepper
4 cups diced cooked chicken breasts
3 cups grated Monterey Jack cheese

In a large soup pot, combine the beans, chicken broth, garlic and half the onions and bring to a boil. Reduce the heat and simmer until the beans are very soft, 3 hours or more. Add more chicken broth if necessary.

In a skillet, sauté the remaining onions in the oil until tender. Add the chiles and seasonings and mix thoroughly; add to the bean mixture. Add the chicken and continue to simmer for 1 hour. Serve topped with the grated cheese and pass squares of warm corn bread.

NOTE: *This is the mellowest chili in the batch, and it is marvelous, but I put out lots of jalapeños and chopped onions with it, too. And— surprise!—Tabasco.*

MIKE'S SINGLE-MALT SPARERIBS

Too crude for an actual recipe, more technique, but so good.

Allow 1 pound ribs per person.

Preheat the oven to 350°F.

Slather big meaty ribs (cut apart) in your favorite barbecue sauce (bottled or homemade) and liberal doses of Lea & Perrins Worcestershire Sauce. Wrap in foil and bake for 30 minutes.

Remove from the foil, save the juices, and take the ribs out to the grill. Cook over medium coals for 30 minutes more, basting with this mixture: lots of orange marmalade, chopped garlic, a big slug of scotch (the name of this recipe aside, I wouldn't break open the Macallans for this; anything drinkable will do), and ground ginger. Cook until crusty and blackened.

To the remaining marmalade mixture add the reserved juices (fat drained if you wish) and another slug of scotch, and pass as a sauce.

By the way, if you've never cooked *lamb* riblets, they are very savory and succulent, just smaller and cheaper. Prepare the same way, adding Pickapeppa sauce to the barbecue sauce mixture—or not. Roast for 20 minutes, then finish on the grill as above, basting and glazing with a mixture of melted mint jelly, crushed garlic, and lemon juice. A jolt of bourbon, as with the scotch and the pork, improves the situation even more, which is awfully good to begin with.

THE FREMONT FIRE DEPARTMENT'S CENSORED SAUSAGE AND STUFFING STEW

This book is far too genteel for me to tell you what the Bravest of Fremont, Ohio, actually call this dish, but when it's my cousin Tim Grayson's turn to cook, this is what the guys request, although by its other name. As Fireman Tim cheerfully comments, "Looks like hell but tastes great!" And yes, I am assuming, as must be you, that he at least doubles this recipe—Fremont's not *that* small.

SERVES 4

> 1 pound *hot* pork sausage (hey, it's the fire department)
> Stove Top stuffing, any flavor (the FFD likes corn bread)
> 1 large onion, chopped
> Two 16-ounce cans creamed corn
> 1 teaspoon pepper
> 1 tablespoon chopped parsley

Dig out the 1974 Rival Crockpot from the back of the closet (remember, this is a Republican cookbook).

In a large skillet, brown the sausage. Drain the fat and add 1 cup of the stuffing mix (reserve the seasoning packet). Spoon the sausage and stuffing into the bottom of the crockpot. Combine all the other ingredients and pour into the pot.

Mix the seasoning packet from the stuffing with 1½ cups water and pour over the top. Cover and cook on high for 2 hours, or on low for 3 to 4 hours. (If you were not a bride at some point during the Nixon or Ford administrations, and therefore did not receive a Rival Crockpot as a wedding present, you can bake in a 325°F. oven for 1 hour.)

LUSTY LAMB SHANKS WITH LEMONY LIMAS

My godmother, Mildred, used to play golf at The Club all day, then fly into the kitchen about half an hour before my godfather got home from the office. She'd chop a couple of onions, throw them into a pot with some butter, and scramble into a shower and some wifely clothes. When my godfather walked in the door, it smelled as if she'd been cooking for hours. He never caught on.

This dish has that same effect: You can put it together very quickly, then let it simmer for hours, making your kitchen smell like a Tuscan farmhouse kitchen. Which is especially appropriate if, instead of tending the stove all day, you have been out purchasing Tuscan products (can you spell P-R-A-D-A?). By the way, if you do it in a crockpot you can keep the illusion going for at least 10 hours (5 on high, 5 on low) and you don't have to brown anything.

SERVES 4

4 big meaty lamb shanks, seasoned with salt and pepper
2 tablespoons olive oil
1 big onion, sliced
5 big garlic cloves, smashed
1½ teaspoons fragrant thyme
1½ teaspoons oregano
1 big lemon, or 2 small, sliced paper thin
Two 10-ounce packages frozen lima beans, thawed by running
    cold water over them in a colander
1 bottle good red wine
Chopped parsley, for garnish (optional)
Chopped scallions, for garnish (optional)

In a flameproof casserole big enough to hold them comfortably, brown the shanks in the olive oil. Add the onion, garlic, thyme, and oregano and sauté for 2 to 3 minutes. Scatter the lemon slices over, add the lima beans (okay if partly frozen), then pour in the wine. Bring to a boil, lower to a bare simmer, and cover. Cook for 2½ to 3 hours, stirring occasionally if you happen to be home. Check to see if the meat is so tender it is falling off the bone; if not, cook until it is. You can uncover for the last of the cooking if you want the sauce to reduce.

(If using a crockpot, put all ingredients in the cold pot and turn on high for 5 hours. Remove the lid and, working quickly, give it a stir to move the meat around, cover again, and turn down to low for another 5.)

Skim the fat (or refrigerate overnight and then lift off as much hardened fat as your cardiac condition dictates), then taste for seasoning, adding salt and pepper if needed.

Garnish with lots of rough-chopped parsley and, of course, chopped scallions. You will want some crusty peasanty bread to soak up the sauce.

FAST AND FANCY VEAL CHOPS

Serve these with a favorite green salad and Hot Damn Peaches (page 107), which for some mystical reason taste especially good with this.

SERVES 4, YET AGAIN REGRETTABLY EXPENSIVELY, BUT SO MEMORABLY

MARINADE

¼ cup good overpriced olive oil
3 tablespoons overpriced balsamic vinegar
1 tablespoon soy sauce (you'll have to shop around for an overpriced brand)
3 big garlic cloves, smashed and chopped
Lots of freshly ground black pepper

4 big prime loin veal chops, about 1 inch thick, overpriced and undertrimmed

Preheat the broiler. Mix the marinade ingredients in a glass dish or resealable plastic bag.

Marinate the chops for at least 15 minutes while you mix the martinis and the broiler heats. Longer is okay, but not much more than 1 hour.

Remove the chops from the marinade and pat dry. Discard the marinade.

Broil the chops for 10 minutes on the first side, then turn and broil for 6 minutes more. Cut into the meat to check for doneness; meat that expensive should still be pink, not gray.

CHAPTER SEVEN

G.O.PEAS AND OTHER CHOSEN SIDES

R epublicans love vegetables, but only if cooked until everyone is quite sure they're dead. Which is why you won't find many Republicans nibbling on raw edamame beans or asking for seconds on the seaweed salad. Instead, they fill up the other side of that plate with My Mom's R.I.P. Green Beans and Bacon; Rush's Mom's Fluffy Potato Casserole; Dad's Corn Pudding/Soufflé; Hot Damn Peaches; Skaneateles Potatoes; Miss Scarlett's Saltine Salad; Susie Townsend's Ex-Husband's Sesame Broccoli Pasta Salad, Significantly Improved; and a dozen or so more easy-does-it dishes to ride shotgun with that roast beef.

MY MOM'S R.I.P. GREEN BEANS AND BACON

As the only Grayson who ever moved to New York (or ever would in a million years), I used to feel it my duty to return home to St. Louis and raise my family's consciousness with cutting-edge culinary concepts like fresh, crisp, undercooked green beans. That lasted about five minutes, and you know what? They were right.

Trimming and stringing the green beans is a perfect job for the little kids in the family who don't know any better. Make them compete. Trust me, it works (and sometimes works well enough to extend the game to shucking corn).

SERVES 4

> ¼ pound good smoky slab bacon, rind on if possible (or strip
>   bacon, cut up)
> 2 pounds green beans, trimmed and stringed
> 1 big onion, sliced vertically
> 2 cups chicken broth (canned is fine)

Cut the bacon into chunks and in a big pot barely sauté it, just to release the fat and flavor. Add the beans, onion, and chicken broth and cook, covered, over medium heat, for at least 1 hour, could be 2, or until the beans have turned a sort of grim grayish-green and are lying there, limp and lifeless, but (aha!) *melting luxuriously and lusciously into the onions and bacon.* If there is a meager residue of broth, by now a rich and intensely flavored sauce, it means they are done, quite dead—and perfect. *Damn,* these are good!

RUSH'S MOM'S FLUFFY POTATO CASSEROLE

No wonder the Limbaugh boys are such fierce overachievers: they grew up on staunch Republican food like this. David, the columnist and author; Rush, the, well, The Rush; and cousin Steve, the chief justice of the supreme court of Missouri, ate this Millie Limbaugh family favorite at every major national holiday, and look how they turned out.

Now. While I am the last person on earth to take on a Limbaugh, any Limbaugh, I feel it my duty to tell you that "fluffy" is not the first word that comes to mind when one is devouring this dish. Fabulous, fearsome, fantastic, yes, but I have yet to think "fluffy" while greedily slogging through all that butter, cream cheese, and sour cream. But my, oh me, oh EIB, is it good.

SERVES 8 TO 10

> 8 to 10 medium Idaho potatoes
> Garlic salt, powder, or granules, even fresh!
> Salt and pepper
> 1 stick (8 tablespoons) butter or oleo, or more to taste
> Milk
> One 8-ounce package cream cheese
> 1 cup sour cream
> Paprika

Preheat oven to 350°F.

Peel and quarter the potatoes and boil until done. Season with garlic, salt, pepper, and butter or oleo and mash (Rush's mom used an electric hand mixer; you can also do it in a food mill). Use enough milk to make the potatoes a little thinner than mashed potatoes. Beat the cream cheese and sour cream together and add to the potatoes.

Place in a greased casserole dish and top with pats of butter and paprika. Bake for 30 minutes or until hot.

This may be refrigerated for 3 days before baking or frozen for up to 6 months. I know, but that's what Millie said.

SKANEATELES POTATOES

This is another nonrecipe, but a great way to prepare potatoes, especially for a big crowd. I first tasted them at somebody else's family reunion on New York's Lake Skaneateles, where they were cooked in a huge, beat-up pot and served in big bowls as finger food. They are killer.

Cook small unpeeled new potatoes in boiling salted water in a huge, beat-up pot until just done, but not mushy. Pour out the water, then add enough coarse salt to cover the bottom of the pot liberally (sorry—slip of the tongue). Put the pot and potatoes back on the heat and shake the pot until the potatoes are dried and crispy and dusted with salt. Pour out into big bowls and serve with melted butter, sour cream with lots of chives, or your favorite vinaigrette. Make thousands.

DAD'S CORN PUDDING/SOUFFLÉ

Dad wasn't much for fussing. He liked things simple, and things don't get much simpler than this pudding, one of those one-of-everything things. But he was justifiably very proud of it, enough so that in later years, he took to calling it a soufflé, despite his lifelong mistrust of the French.

SERVES 4

1 can cream-style corn
1 cup milk
1 cup crushed cracker crumbs (When a
    Republican says crackers, he
    means Premium Saltines. When
    he means Ritz crackers, he says
    Ritz crackers, and so on.)
1 egg, beaten
1 onion, chopped
Salt and pepper
Dash of nutmeg

Preheat the oven to 350°F.

Mix all the ingredients together and pour into a greased baking dish. Bake for 30 minutes. Great with any meat, especially pork.

GAYLE'S MASHED CORN

This dish used to go by the romantic and evocative name "Hot Corn Casserole." It was changed in honor of our friend Gayle, who, while making it for the first time, read the recipe carelessly, and instead of mashing the RO✱TEL tomatoes, spent a frantic half hour mashing the two cans of whole kernel corn with a rolling pin, turning her kitchen into a sticky yellow corn-confettied hell. I would be remiss if I failed to mention Gayle is *not* a Republican.

This is great alongside anything Tex-Mex. Also anything else.

SERVES 6 TO 8 AS A SIDE DISH

> 2 tablespoons butter or margarine, melted
> ¼ cup whole milk
> One 8-ounce package cream cheese, softened
> One 10-ounce can RO✱TEL tomatoes, diced, or mashed if using whole
> ¼ teaspoon salt
> ¼ teaspoon garlic salt
> ¼ teaspoon crushed red pepper flakes
> Two 15-ounce cans whole kernel corn, drained

Preheat the oven to 350°F.

In a large bowl, combine the melted butter and the milk. Add the softened cream cheese. Drain the tomatoes and add, then add the salt, garlic salt, and red pepper flakes. Mix well, taste, and adjust the seasonings. Add the corn. Pour into a buttered 8 × 12-inch baking dish and bake for 30 minutes.

MISS SCARLETT'S MARINATED SALTINE SALAD

This is as Southern as Tara (and my aunt Nellie Jo), and it shows. I think it unlikely you find one member of the Writers Guild of America, East, who would crush up a bunch of Saltines, add Miracle Whip, and call it salad, but I also dare you to find any dish in the Kerry Family Cookbook that tastes anywhere near as good.

This is a great side dish, a great picnic dish, or a great dish to make when you stumble, sniveling, into the kitchen in your flannel pajamas, feeling sorry for yourself. And even with the scallions, it's a kid-pleaser.

SERVES 6, AND MULTIPLIES EASILY FOR A CROWD

> 1 sleeve Premium Saltines (not the oxymoronically named unsalted Saltines)
> 1 cup Miracle Whip, or mayonnaise, depending on where you were brought up
> 1 big ripe summer tomato, chopped, or 1 cup cherry tomatoes, halved
> 1 bunch green onions, chopped (yes, Aunt Nellie Jo knew Yankees call them scallions, which is, of course, precisely why she did not)
> 2 hard-boiled eggs, chopped
> Garlic salt and black pepper to taste
> Crisp crumbled bacon, for garnish (optional)
> Tabasco sauce standing by

In a big bowl, coarsely crush the crackers with your hands, leaving good-size pieces. Add everything else but the bacon and Tabasco and mix well. Refrigerate overnight. Garnish with the bacon and serve, or say to hell with the bacon and eat it right out of the bowl.

EUGENIA GIORDANO'S INGENIOUS LIME CUCUMBER SALAD

What would a Republican cookbook be without a lime Jell-O salad? Jean Giordano obliges, but then so does my sister, in a recipe that follows.

The fact is, lime Jell-O, like Lipton soup mix, and certain other iconic items abundantly represented in this book, reflect a certain Republican zeitgeist, an almost tangible collective consciousness every real Republican taps into at some point or another, no matter how evolved she may believe she is. Which is why this may be the only cookbook you will ever own that has two—count 'em, two—lime Jell-O recipes in one cookbook.

Is this a great party, or what?

SERVES 6

> One 3-ounce package lime Jell-O
> ¾ cup hot water
> ¼ cup fresh lemon juice
> 1 teaspoon onion juice
> 1 cup chopped, unpeeled cucumber
> 1 cup sour cream or mayonnaise
> Lettuce, for serving

Dissolve the gelatin in the hot water. Add the lemon and onion juices. Chill until partly set. Fold in the cucumber and sour cream. Pour into 6 oiled individual molds and chill until firm. Unmold on crisp lettuce.

AUNT SHARI'S GREEN STUFF

Née Mrs. Manley's 7-Up Salad, this jiggling electric-green mainstay of the Grayson family Thanksgiving has officially been re-named for my sister, who, having made it every Thanksgiving for twenty-five years, deserves her due. We make fun of it—in fact, the very title is a cleaned-up version of what the older kids actually call it—but nobody ever passes it up. I don't know anything about Mrs. Manley other than that there can be no doubt whatsoever she was a Republican. Just get a load of that Cool Whip.

7 ounces 7-Up
One 3-ounce package lime Jell-O
19 large marshmallows (not 18, not 20—who knows?)
One 8-ounce package Philadelphia cream cheese, softened
One 20-ounce can crushed pineapple (juice-packed)
¾ cup chopped pecans
One 8-ounce container Cool Whip

In a medium saucepan, heat the 7-Up, then add the lime Jell-O and stir until it dissolves. Add the marshmallows and stir until they are similarly dispatched. In a mixing bowl, pour the hot Jell-O mixture over the cream cheese, thereby destroying a perfectly good bagel spread and creating instead a greenish slimy goo. Stir in the pineapple and its juice along with the nuts. Cover and place the dish behind several tall objects in the refrigerator, to hide it from view in case the tiramasù police stop by. When it is partially set, fold in the Cool Whip. Chill completely and serve, but only to people to whom you are related by blood or marriage.

WORLD'S BEST SLAW

This is another of my mother's recipes, and I have never met anyone in my whole life who didn't agree with its name. It is imperative alongside anything barbecued, especially pork, which my father loved so much he turned several acres of our country house/farm/cattle ranch/tax write-off into a pig factory, which every spring produced adorable little squealing examples of The Other White Meat, thrilling the adorable little squealing examples of Republican grandchildren no end. As it was at the remotest corner of the property, it worked fine for a while, except when the wind blew the wrong way.

Incidentally, my mother, who is legally blind, shreds her own cabbage in mere seconds on a primitive, razor-sharp, death-defying mandoline, which she bought at a flea market for a dollar more than forty years ago. It, and her using it, terrifies me, and she considers me a complete wuss because it does. She is right. I am a wuss, and she is not.

1 large head of cabbage, shredded very fine
2 red onions, also shredded fine
1 tablespoon celery seed (not celery salt), or more if it seems
    skimpy
¾ cup sugar
½ cup vinegar
½ cup vegetable oil
1 to 2 tablespoons mustard (yellow is the original, but Dijon is
    better, I think)
1½ teaspoons salt

In a large bowl, toss the cabbage and onions well with your hands. Sprinkle in the celery seed—it should be visible, but not overwhelming. Chill.

In a small saucepan, combine all the other ingredients and bring to boil. Pour over the cold cabbage mixture.

If you serve this immediately you get the hot dressing and the crisp cold slaw, which is delicious dynamite. But hold on: The leftovers are equally good, marinated into sweet and sour succulence, and fabulous, especially on pork barbecue sandwiches or just piled onto toasted or grilled bread.

MOM'S MEAN BEANS

The evil twin of World's Best Slaw. In our family, these two usually travel in tandem.

SERVES 10 OR SO

DRAIN AND PUT INTO A LARGE CASSEROLE

One 16-ounce can kidney beans
One 16-ounce can butter or lima beans
One 16-ounce can black beans
Two 16-ounce cans pork and beans

(The truth is, you can use whatever beans you like for the first three, canned or frozen, but approximately in these amounts. The pork and beans are less negotiable.)

POUROVER SAUCE

½ pound bacon, cut up
4 onions, sliced
8 big garlic cloves, smashed and chopped
1 cup brown sugar
2 teaspoons dry mustard
½ cup cider vinegar
Salt and freshly ground black pepper to taste

Preheat the oven to 350°F.

Cook the bacon until almost crisp, remove from the skillet, and reserve. Sauté the onions and garlic in the bacon fat until soft, then add the rest of the ingredients. Simmer for 15 minutes, then pour over the beans and bake for 60 to 90 minutes, it really doesn't matter. When it smells irresistible, top with the reserved bacon and serve. Alongside that slaw!

McCAIN'S MEAN BEANS

I'm not trying to get competitive here, but the senator deserves equal time for his beans, and since my mom always votes for him anyway, it seems fair to me. The senator serves these with anything barbecued.

SERVES 4 TO 6

1 medium onion, chopped
1 teaspoon butter
One 16-ounce can red kidney beans
One 16-ounce can D&M baked beans
1 cup ketchup
1 cup packed brown sugar
1 teaspoon vinegar
1 teaspoon yellow French's mustard
4 strips of fried bacon, cooled and crumbled

Preheat the oven to 350°F.

In a skillet, sauté the chopped onion in the butter. In a large baking pot, combine the kidney beans, D&M baked beans, ketchup, brown sugar, vinegar, mustard, and crumbled bacon. Add the sautéed onions and mix well.

Bake covered for 35 minutes, or until piping hot.

KEITH'S BAKED ONIONS

This is like onion soup on the hoof (see Note); a bull's-eye side dish for any kind of meat, especially big rare steaks. So stupid-easy, so good, and nobody, nobody, nobody doesn't like it. You will be grovelingly grateful for this recipe.

1 big white onion per person
1 beef bouillon cube per person
Unsalted butter
Heavy-duty aluminum foil

Preheat the oven to 350°F.

Peel the onions, but do not cut off the root end. Cut a wedge-shaped well in the top end, big enough to put a bouillon cube in—and put a bouillon cube in. Top with about 1 teaspoon of unsalted butter. Wrap each onion loosely in a square of aluminum foil and twist the top to close.

Put the foil-wrapped onions in a baking dish and bake for 1 hour or so. Longer is fine if you're behind on everything else. To serve, place each onion, still wrapped, in a small shallow bowl. When the foil is removed (and just wait until you get that first whiff of their aroma), there will appear a wonderfully soft onion in a puddle of rich broth.

NOTE: *Serve these with grilled baguette slices rubbed with garlic and topped with grated Gruyère cheese, then broiled until the cheese browns, and it* will *actually taste like the most delicious onion soup you never got to be insulted in Paris for.*

SECTION FOUR SUMMER SQUASH

A "section," on Missouri maps, is a piece of farmland measuring one square mile. Around late August, if you are not careful, the whole of this square mile will be entirely taken over by zucchini. This recipe dates from the happy days of our family's aforementioned weekend getaway, cleverly named Section Four (its technical designation on the map of Greene County), and was created by my mother as a way to use up some of the mutant monster squashes terrorizing the rest of the garden.

As in many Republican recipes, especially the old-fashioned ones like this, the proportions are up to the cook, depending on how much zucchini needs to be Selected Out.

Zucchini or yellow summer squash
Onions
Granulated chicken broth mix
Baco Bits

Chunk up the squash and chop up a lot of onions. Sprinkle with chicken broth mix and Baco Bits. Yes, of course you can use real chopped cooked bacon, but it doesn't taste like Section Four then.

Cook covered in a large saucepan in a small amount of water until soft and Republican-mushy.

NOTE: *Wonderful on lazy summer nights, especially when keeping company with those lush August tomatoes, cucumbers, and onion slices that have been marinating in vinegar and water since late July. At Section Four, there was a large crock of them being constantly topped up, and eaten at almost every meal.*

EVELYN'S SPINACH CHEDDAR CASSEROLE

Another dish without which A Good Old Republican Thanksgiving or Christmas would be unthinkable, and for which Evelyn doubles or triples this recipe, depending on who's coming.

SERVES 4 TO 6

> One 10-ounce package frozen chopped spinach
> 1 cup cooked rice (yes, of course, we use Minute)
> 1 cup shredded Cheddar cheese
> 2 eggs, beaten
> 2 tablespoons melted butter
> 1/3 cup milk
> 1/2 cup sliced scallions
> 1 teaspoon Worcestershire sauce
> 1 teaspoon salt
> 1/4 teaspoon crushed dried rosemary (or 1 tablespoon fresh, chopped)

Preheat the oven to 350°F.

Thaw the spinach by running cold water over it in a fine sieve, and drain very well. Combine the spinach with the cooked rice and cheese, add all other ingredients, and stir to mix well. Pour into a greased casserole and bake for 25 to 30 minutes.

HOT DAMN PEACHES

These are dumb-and-dumber delicious, marvelous with any grilled meat, especially Fast and Fancy Veal Chops (page 93).

SERVES 2 TO 3

Sesame seeds, about ½ to 1 teaspoon per peach half
One 15-ounce can peach halves, freestones preferably
One .7-ounce package Good Seasons Italian dressing dry mix
¼ cup grated sharp Cheddar cheese

Preheat the broiler.

Put the sesame seeds in a hot, dry skillet and stand there, shaking the pan, until they start to brown and are popping at you (one of those round screen things from The Anal-Compulsives' Homemade Tortilla Chips, page 16, is useful here). Or, you can do as I do and go answer the phone or the door, forget about them, and ruin the first batch as they become a sodden blackened mess. It sometimes takes me three batches to deliver one.

Sprinkle the peach halves with the dry seasoning, fill the cavities with grated cheese, and sprinkle sesame seeds over. Watching even more carefully than you watched the sesame seeds, stick the peaches under the broiler until the cheese melts and blisters and the seeds are browner still. These are too silly to be this good, but they are.

RICK THE BACHELOR'S GREEN CHILE RICE

For a long time, this was my brother Rick's favorite dish to impress girlfriends with. In truth, it was the only dish he knew how to make, but he understood intuitively that if he could make this, throw a couple of steaks on the grill, and get her to make the salad (girls love to make salads at guys' apartments), there'd be dinner.

And possibly dessert.

2 cups sour cream
2 cups cooked rice
Salt
½ pound sharp Cheddar cheese, or Monterey Jack, cut into
      domino-size strips
One 6-ounce can mild green chiles, drained and cut into strips
Butter
½ cup grated Cheddar, Monterey Jack, or Parmesan cheese
Chopped scallions, for garnish

Preheat the oven to 350°F.

Mix the sour cream into the rice, and add salt to taste. Butter a casserole, and spread half of the rice mixture on the bottom. Wrap the cheese strips in the chile strips and scatter over, then top with the rest of the rice. Dot the top lavishly with butter and sprinkle with the grated cheese. Bake uncovered for 30 minutes, scatter scallions over, and serve immediately to that nubile young woman over there tossing the romaine.

GREEN CHILE PASTA

Zippy and zingy, and almost too substantial to be called a side. But a very different way to do pasta, and hard to stop eating.

SERVES 6

6 thick slices bacon, diced (or more if you like—I do)
8 ounces vermicelli, or other really skinny pasta, broken into 2-inch
    pieces
1 huge onion, chopped
3 big garlic cloves, smashed and chopped
One 4-ounce can diced green California chiles
One 14½-ounce can College Inn beef broth
One 1-pound can Italian tomatoes, crushed
2 tablespoons red wine vinegar
Big dose of dried oregano, crushed to release the flavor
Salt and freshly ground black pepper to taste
Freshly grated Parmesan cheese

In a 3- or 4-quart flameproof casserole, cook the bacon over medium heat until crisp. Remove and reserve. To the drippings (about ¼ cup worth—if there is more, discard), add the broken-up pasta, onion, and garlic and sauté until all are golden brown. Add the chiles, beef broth, tomatoes, vinegar, oregano, salt, and pepper and stir well. Cover and simmer until the pasta is tender and most of the liquid is absorbed, about 15 minutes.

Serve hot, passing the Parmesan.

MAGI'S BAKED GNOCCHI

Magi Durham Ziff has run a fabled poker game every other Wednesday night in New York for thirty-three years even though she no longer lives in New York. How does she do it? By maintaining a studio apartment in the city solely for that purpose, furnished only with a Murphy bed, a poker table, and a state-of-the-art miniature kitchen. You wouldn't believe what comes out of that kitchen to feed her poker players, including these gnocchi, which she went all the way to Italy to learn how to make. Obviously this recipe is for when you want to pass for a Democrat, as no self-respecting Republican I know would ever make her own gnocchi, even if she knew what it was.

SERVES 4

1 quart milk
1 cup water
1⅜ sticks (11 tablespoons)
    unsalted butter
1 tablespoon salt
½ pound semolina
½ pound Gorgonzola cheese
Freshly grated Parmigiano-Reggiano cheese

Preheat the oven to 350°F.

Pour the milk and water into a large pot and bring to a boil. Add 1 stick of the butter and the salt and then whisk in the semolina, whisking constantly to prevent lumps. Cook for 5 minutes.

Pour the mixture onto a flat work surface and, using a spatula, level the surface to about ½-inch thickness. Cut into small squares.

Place the gnocchi (for indeed, that's what you have now) in a buttered baking pan, cover with pats of Gorgonzola, and dust with Parmigiano. Dot with the remaining butter and bake for 10 minutes, or until golden.

SUSIE TOWNSEND'S EX-HUSBAND'S SESAME BROCCOLI PASTA SALAD, SIGNIFICANTLY IMPROVED

Now, this is a famous recipe, because it was actually cooked off in a Gilroy Garlic Festival Great Garlic Cook-off, one of only eight national finalists. I know, because I was there Cooking it Off. It was only when I didn't win, place, or show that my disappointed and disgusted twelve-year-old son, who had sat stoically in the viewing bleachers the whole long morning, pointed out to his mother, Girl Ad Biggie, the suddenly, sadly obvious: "Mom, you forgot to put the name of the product in the headline."

SERVES 6 TO 8

    8 garlic cloves, smashed and chopped
    2 teaspoons Asian sesame oil (the dark kind)
    ½ cup soy sauce
    1 teaspoon honey
    1 tablespoon hot Chinese chile-garlic paste
    ¼ cup white vinegar
    1 tablespoon coarsely ground fresh black pepper
    1 pound penne, rigatoni, or fusilli, cooked just until dente, drained
        and kept warm
    1 head of broccoli, separated into florets, steamed until just crisp-
        tender
    1 bunch of scallions, trimmed and chopped, white and green parts
        all
    Garlic salt to taste
    ½ cup sesame seeds, toasted in a dry skillet over medium heat

Make the dressing: Sauté the garlic in the sesame oil just until slightly softened, then whisk together with the soy sauce, honey, chile-garlic paste, vinegar, and pepper.

Toss with the pasta, broccoli, and scallions. Taste for seasoning and add garlic salt as you wish. Add the sesame seeds and toss again, combining thoroughly.

Change name of recipe to Susie Townsend's Ex-Husband's Sesame Broccoli Salad, Significantly Improved with Fresh Garlic, Garlic Paste, and Garlic Salt. Resubmit to Gilroy Garlic Festival next year.

AND FINALLY, DID YOU KNOW THAT IF YOU . . .

. . . peel and seed cucumbers, cut them into non-cucumber shapes, and sauté them in butter, nobody will know they are cucumbers, but will love them? And when you salt them and sprinkle them with dill they are great with anything seafood, especially salmon?

. . . trim scallions, and lay them in a skillet with ½ inch of boiling water with some butter, chopped lemon, and chopped almonds, cover and cook, they are drop-dead elegant beside any aged steak? And if you remove the scallions from the skillet after only 30 seconds and reduce the sauce down, they are even better?

. . . sauté cherry tomatoes in some butter and garlic until they collapse and get all wrinkly, and have a lot of chopped basil or parsley or dill standing by, they are beautiful and delicious with roast meat or chicken?

. . . toss cauliflower florets sliced about ¼ inch thick in olive oil, garlic salt, cumin, and crushed red pepper flakes and roast at 450° F. until they are browned and somewhat crispy (turning once), they don't taste as much like cauliflower as they do like some exotic meaty garlic potato chip?

. . . toss steamed Brussels sprouts (Brussels sprouts???) in a mixture of sesame oil, soy sauce, white vinegar, scallions, and toasted sesame seeds, even little kids and cranky old men will eat them? And that they are even better cold, having marinated in all the above?

CHAPTER EIGHT

YOU CAN'T MAKE A BLOODY MARY WITHOUT BREAKING EGGS,
and Fourteen Other Reasons Republicans Love Brunch

▪▪ ★

Besides being an excellent excuse to start drinking early, brunch is also a tactful way to nudge weekend guests back to the city in a timely fashion ("Now, you simply *can't* leave until after brunch!"). This leaves the rest of Sunday for fun and wholesome Republican family activities, such as gathering in front of the TV to watch the golf or, in the off-season, watch Republican movies on TCM (hint: *The Legend of Bagger Vance* is a Republican movie; *All the President's Men* is not).

CARL'S FAMOUS NIGHT-BEFORE BRUNCH

Carl Stewart is a good cook, but he is an even better bartender, and this do-ahead recipe frees him up for the really important work of mixing bottomless pitchers of brunch-appropriate beverages (see The Anemic Mary on page 7 and The Salty Yaller Dawg on page 6). Those, this, and a salad whipped up by the designated driver should get everybody up and out, one way or another, by two.

SERVES 8

> 16 slices white bread, crusts cut off and lightly buttered
> 2 cups cubed cooked ham, or 1 pound cooked and drained breakfast sausage
> 8 ounces sharp Cheddar cheese, grated
> 6 chopped scallions
> 8 eggs
> 3½ cups milk
> 1 teaspoon dry mustard
> 1 teaspoon salt
> 2 cups crushed cornflakes
> 1 stick (8 tablespoons) butter, melted

Butter a 9 × 12-inch baking dish. Place half the buttered bread in the bottom and sprinkle with the ham, cheese, and scallions. Top with the rest of the bread. Beat together the eggs, milk, mustard, and salt. Pour over the bread. Cover with foil and refrigerate overnight.

Preheat the oven to 350°F. and remove the casserole from the fridge.

About 1 hour before serving, take it out, sprinkle the casserole with the cornflakes, and pour on the melted butter. Bake for 1 hour.

MAJORITY RULES CHILE CHEESE SOUFFLÉ

Senate Majority Leader Bill Frist, M.D., a world-renowned heart transplant surgeon, performs open-can surgery on some California chiles to create this favorite family brunch dish for Karyn and the boys, Harrison, Jonathan, and Bryan.

SERVES 6

> 3 cans whole green chiles, cut into strips
> 3 cups plus ½ cup sharp Cheddar cheese, finely grated
> 2 cups milk
> 4 eggs, beaten
> ¾ cup flour

Preheat the oven to 325°F.

Layer the chiles and cheese twice in a 9 × 12-inch casserole dish. Mix the milk, eggs, and flour and pour over the chiles and cheese. Cover the dish with aluminum foil and let set for 10 minutes, then bake for 1 hour. Remove the cover and bake for another 15 minutes.

LOBSTER EGGS BENEDICT WITH SALLY DANFORTH'S LEMONY HOLLANDAISE SAUCE

This is a shamefully showoff dish, for weekend guests who happen to have a posh country/beach/South of France house to which you would not mind being invited. Sally would not stoop so low (I would), but her Hollandaise is the easiest and most delicious I have ever made, so she is tarred with this brush.

SERVES 4 ADULTS BECAUSE LOBSTER IS EXPENSIVE AND THE CHILDREN LIKE PEANUT BUTTER BETTER ANYWAY

> Two 2-pound lobsters, cooked however you cook them (the way I
>   cook them is to call Citarella and ask them to have them ready
>   in an hour)
> 4 English muffins, split, toasted, and buttered lightly
> 4 poached eggs
> Sally Danforth's Lemony Hollandaise Sauce (recipe follows)

Remove the lobster meat from the shells and pile sliced lobster meat generously onto each muffin half; top with poached eggs and Hollandaise sauce.

SALLY DANFORTH'S LEMONY HOLLANDAISE SAUCE

6 egg yolks
4 tablespoons fresh lemon juice
2 sticks (1 cup) unsalted butter, cut into small pieces
Salt and pepper to taste

In a saucepan mix together the egg yolks and lemon juice, place over very low heat, and add half of the butter. Stir constantly with a wire whisk. When the butter is melted, gradually add the rest of the butter and continue stirring until it thickens. Season to taste.

If the sauce begins to curdle, remove from heat and add either another egg yolk or some cream or 1 tablespoon of hot water.

NEW ENGLAND BLUEBERRY JOHNNYCAKES

Another pure Yankee favorite from Mimi Coffin Ragsdale, she of the Mayflower-arriving, Nantucket-founding, FDR-fifteen-cent-stamp-boycotting Coffins (see page 11). More authentically Republican than this it does not get. These are mighty fine with bacon and sausage on the side, but then so are Styrofoam peanuts.

MAKES ABOUT 40

1 cup white cornmeal
1 teaspoon sugar
1/2 teaspoon salt
1 1/2 cups boiling water
3/4 cup blueberries
Vegetable oil, for frying
Butter, for serving
Warm pure maple syrup, for serving

Mix together the cornmeal, sugar, and salt. Add the boiling water and mix well, then gently stir in the blueberries.

Pour a thin layer of vegetable oil in a heavy frying pan and heat until a drop of water spits at you. Put tablespoonish-size dollops of batter into the pan and *"leave for six minutes before turning!"* (Her emphasis, and I wouldn't mess with her.) Turn over and cook for about the same time on the other side, or until golden.

Serve 3 to 4 per person with butter and warm maple syrup.

BOB DOLE'S KANSAS WHOLE WHEAT HONEY BREAD

They've got an awful lot of wheat in Russell, Kansas, but a little less when the senator whips up a batch of this terrific bread. Great therapy for when he's feeling homesick, or for when Elizabeth is working late at the office. Look, in a two-senator family, everybody's got to pitch in.

MAKES 2 LOAVES, 1 FOR EVERY SENATOR IN
YOUR MARRIAGE

1 cake yeast
1½ cups lukewarm water
2 cups milk
1 tablespoon shortening
¼ cup honey
1 tablespoon salt
2 cups sifted flour
4 cups whole wheat flour

Soften the yeast in the lukewarm water. Scald the milk and add the shortening, honey, and salt. Pour into a large bowl and add the softened yeast and the flour. Knead well, transfer to a large greased bowl, cover with greased plastic wrap, and let rise in a warm place until doubled in bulk. Punch down and shape into loaves. Place in greased loaf pans. Cover and let rise until doubled in bulk. Bake at 375°F. for 1 great-smelling hour.

CRISTYNE'S BIG-APPLE-GOES-BANANAS BANANA BREAD

The only hard part about this recipe is trying to figure out when Cristyne (Lategano-Nicholas) ever finds time to make it. As president and C.E.O. of NYC&CO, the official convention and tourism department of New York City, Cristyne spends most of her days doing stuff like snagging the 2004 Republican Convention for New York—the triumphant announcement of which, not surprisingly, triggered a massive spike in Zoloft sales in certain zip codes in the city, particularly those of the Upper Left Side. But then, Cristyne is used to provoking anxiety among less Republican-oriented New Yorkers; she was Rudy's director of communications during his first term, and, as we all know, he had a lot to say. And believe me, so does Cristyne.

MAKES 1 LOAF

> 3 ripe mashed bananas
> ³⁄₄ cup sugar
> 1 egg
> ¹⁄₄ teaspoon salt
> ¹⁄₂ stick (4 tablespoons) melted butter
> 1 teaspoon baking soda
> 1 tablespoon water
> 2 cups sifted flour
> ¹⁄₂ cup chopped walnuts (optional)

Preheat the oven to 350°F.

Spray a 9 × 5 × 3-inch loaf pan. Mash the bananas in a large bowl. Add the sugar, egg, and salt. Stir in the melted butter.

Combine the baking soda and water in a small bowl and add it to the banana mixture.

Then add the flour and fold in the walnuts, if using. Pour into a greased baking pan. Bake for 55 minutes, or until a toothpick comes out clean.

GOVERNOR PATAKI'S EMPIRE APPLE MUFFINS

This is another of the surprises I encountered putting this book together. When I asked the governor's office for a favorite recipe, I somehow expected something . . . tall. Regal. Commanding. *Gubernatorial.* And now, for the rest of my life, every time I see him, my mind will picture the tall, regal, commanding, gubernatorial George Pataki bustling about the kitchen in a cheerful apron, flour on the tip of his nose, humming "I Love New York," as he greases his muffin tins and pours in his batter. It's enough to keep a (Republican) girl voting for him forever.

And so are these muffins.

MAKES 12

2 cups cake flour
1 teaspoon baking powder
½ teaspoon salt
3 tablespoons brown sugar
½ teaspoon baking soda
1 teaspoon cinnamon
¼ teaspoon cardamom
⅛ teaspoon ground cloves
2 tablespoons New York apple cider
¾ cup sour cream
¼ cup milk
2 eggs, lightly beaten
1½ cups Empire apples, peeled and
    coarsely chopped (see Note)

TOPPING

1 cup almonds
¼ cup brown sugar
1 teaspoon ground nutmeg

Preheat the oven to 350°F.

Sift the dry ingredients together into a mixing bowl.

In a separate bowl, whisk together the cider, sour cream, milk, and eggs. Pour the liquid ingredients into the dry ingredients and gently stir together with a wooden spoon.

Fold the apples into the batter and spoon into greased (or paper-lined) muffin tins.

To make the topping, pulverize the almonds, brown sugar, and nutmeg in a food processor. Sprinkle the topping over the muffins and bake for 20 to 25 minutes, until golden and a tester comes out clean.

NOTE: *Empire apples are the luscious love child of the Red Delicious and McIntosh, so they are a great juicy sweet-tart combo. If you can't find them in your market, create your own litter by using a combo of the parents, or just substitute your favorite baking apple.*

KEITH AND LORRAINE

. . . as a certain three-year-old used to pronounce it. Everybody in my family still calls it that.

MAKES 1 QUICHE, SERVING 6

6 thick slices good smoky bacon, cut into thirds
1 tablespoon unsalted butter
1 large sweet onion, thinly sliced
2 garlic cloves, thinly sliced
½ pound Gruyère, or similar cheese, thinly sliced (try half blue for a real jolt)
One 9-inch prepared pie crust, preferably prepared by somebody else, like Pillsbury, Pet-Ritz, or Marie Callender
3 eggs
1 cup half-and-half (or, what the hell, heavy cream)
Salt and freshly ground black pepper

Preheat the oven to 375°F.

In a large skillet, cook the bacon until almost crisp; remove and reserve. Pour out all but 1 tablespoon of the bacon fat, add the butter, and sauté the onion and garlic. Arrange the bacon, onion, garlic, and cheese over the bottom of the pie crust.

In a bowl, beat the eggs, half-and-half, salt, and pepper together and pour over all. Bake for 25 minutes.

Serve with a crisp green salad and a crisp white wine, or, if you are a much-adored three-year-old, chocolate milk.

FRITTATA

What's great about a frittata is that if you have eggs and a refrigerator, you have a frittata any time you feel like one. All sorts of bits and pieces of former meals can become reincarnated as a terrific brunch dish. This recipe starts from scratch, but feel free to throw in leftover almost anything: vegetables, shredded meats, seafood, whatever. The proportion should be 1 to 2 cups of filling per 6 eggs, but you can also make it with just the eggs and a handful or two of fresh herbs. In other words, this too is more method than recipe—as flexible as your number of guests and the size of your skillets. And also, it's just fun to say. FREEEEE . . . TA TA!

SERVES 4, BUT IS ALMOST INFINITELY MULTIPLIABLE

4 slices bacon, or prosciutto, or 4 ounces spicy sausage, chopped
2 tablespoons olive oil, or half oil and half butter
$\frac{1}{2}$ red bell pepper, chopped
1 small onion, chopped
1 or 2 garlic cloves, smashed and chopped
6 scallions, chopped
6 eggs, lightly beaten
$\frac{1}{2}$ cup freshly grated Parmigiano-Reggiano cheese
Tabasco sauce, to pass

Preheat the broiler.

In a large ovenproof skillet, cook the bacon in the olive oil until lightly browned; remove and reserve. Sauté the bell pepper, onion, and garlic until golden, then add the bacon back in. Add the scallions and distribute the ingredients fairly evenly around the bottom of the skillet, then pour the eggs in all at once and leave them alone. Let cook over medium heat until the eggs begin to firm around the edges; as they do so, gently lift the edges to let more egg flow into the bottom to cook. Continue doing this until the dish is just barely set, but still underdone. Sprinkle the cheese over and stick the frittata under the broiler, watching it like a Rumsfeld hawk. When the cheese melts and browns and bubbles, you are there, and most deliciously so.

Serve hot, or, author's choice, at room temperature, with a good crispy white wine and individual bottles of Tabasco sauce.

SOMEBODY'S SAUSAGE CASSEROLE

There is a person out there somewhere who handed me this recipe at the 1996 Grayson Family Reunion. When I dug it out recently to audition it for this section, I realized it was unsigned, bearing only the note "I use this for brunch, and it's great." Well, I used it for brunch and it *was* great, so here it is, the Recipe of the Unknown Grayson. (For a brief moment the chilling thought crossed my mind that this might be from the liberal branch of the family, but then I saw that cream of mushroom soup and I knew we were safe.)

SERVES 4

> 1 pound bulk pork sausage, such as Jones or Jimmy Dean
> 1 tablespoon oil
> 1 cup uncooked Uncle Ben's Long Grain and Wild Rice (reserve
>   seasoning packet)
> ½ cup chopped onion
> 1 cup chopped celery
> 1 green or red bell pepper, chopped
> 2 cloves garlic, smashed and chopped
> One 10¾-ounce can cream of mushroom soup
> 1 empty cream of mushroom soup can of water
> ¼ cup grated Colby or Cheddar cheese

Preheat the oven to 350°F.

In a large skillet, brown the sausage in the oil until cooked through. Remove and reserve. Brown the rice 3 to 5 minutes, adding more oil if necessary. Then add the onion, celery, bell pepper, and garlic and sauté until softened. Add the soup and water and stir in the seasoning mix. Combine well, put into a casserole, and top with the cheese. Bake uncovered for 45 minutes to 1 hour, or until the rice is done.

NOTE TO ATTENDEES OF THE 1996 GRAYSON FAMILY RE-UNION: If you recognize this recipe, as either your own or that of someone you love, please call me immediately, so you can be properly credited in the upcoming Major Motion Picture based on this book. And let me know who you want to play you. Thanks.

THE UNSINKABLE ANNIE GUNN'S WILD RICE PANCAKES WITH SMOKED TROUT AND HORSERADISH CREAM

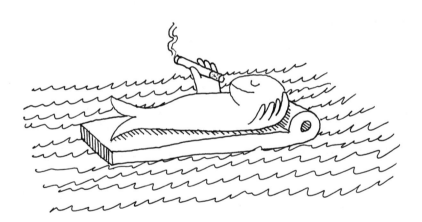

In the summer of 1993, our friend Tom Sehnert appeared in a photo on the front page of *The New York Times* standing on a flat square island, square in the middle of the Missouri River. Turns out the island wasn't an island at all, but the roof of his wildly popular smokehouse, aptly named The Smokehouse, and its equally popular adjoining restaurant, Annie Gunn, in Chesterfield, Missouri, on account of The Smokehouse, Annie, and Tom being up to their wazoos in Missouri River floodwaters, normally twenty miles away. With the river lapping at his loafers, Tom began rebuilding, only to be flooded out again thirty days later. He rebuilt again, defiantly doubling the size of the restaurant. Annie is fictitious, but Tom, his store, and his stubbornness are not. The Missouri state symbol is not a mule for nothing.

SERVES 6

PANCAKES

2 eggs, separated
$\frac{1}{2}$ teaspoon salt
2 cups buttermilk
1 cup flour
1 tablespoon oil
1 teaspoon baking soda
1 tablespoon warm water
3 cups cooked wild rice (don't be afraid—just follow the directions on the package), with 2 tablespoons butter added

HORSERADISH CREAM

1 cup heavy cream, whipped until stiff
$\frac{1}{4}$ cup drained fresh bottled horseradish

6 ounces smoked trout (enough for two thin slices of smoked trout per serving)
Fresh chopped dill or capers, for garnish

In a large bowl, combine the egg yolks, salt, buttermilk, flour, and oil. Whisk to mix well.

In a small bowl, dissolve the baking soda in the warm water; add to the egg mixture. Beat the egg whites in a clean bowl until stiff and fold into the batter. Fold in the wild rice.

Grease well a large griddle or skillet with oil or shortening. Heat until a drop of water sizzles.

Ladle the batter onto the griddle to form small ($\frac{3}{4}$-inch or so) circles. When bubbles form around the edge, peek under to see if the bottom is browned, then flip over for 1 to 2 minutes more (only flip once!).

Combine the whipped cream and horseradish.

Assemble dish: Put a dollop of horseradish cream on each pancake, top with a couple of pieces of smoked trout, sprinkle with fresh chopped dill or capers, and think good thoughts about Lewis and Clark.

MOBY PANCAKE

This is a really easy and dramatic dish that everybody likes, including little kids. If your oven has a window and the oven light isn't burned out like mine usually is, it's sort of fun to watch it happen too, if you have nothing better to do than stare at dough rising.

SERVES 2 TO 3 GENEROUSLY

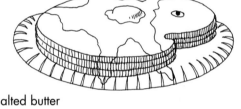

½ cup milk
2 eggs, lightly beaten
Pinch of nutmeg
½ cup flour
1 stick (8 tablespoons) unsalted butter
Juice of ½ lemon
Confectioners' sugar

Preheat the oven to 475°F.

In a bowl, beat together the milk, eggs, nutmeg, and flour, leaving the batter a little lumpy.

When the oven is hot, put the butter in a heavy 12-inch skillet (wrap the handle in foil) and place in the oven. When the butter has melted, immediately pour in the batter.

Return the skillet to the hot oven and watch Moby grow, for 12 to 15 minutes or until puffy and golden.

Remove and sprinkle immediately with the lemon juice and confectioners' sugar, pouring some of the melted butter from the skillet over all.

Topping variations are limitless—brown sugar, maple syrup, fruit syrups, liqueurs, preserves, etc.

OFFICIAL GARLIC GRITS OF THE G.O.P.

Forget every garlic grit you ever knew, this is the real Republican deal. I know, because it comes to me personally from Rosemary Oliver, mother of Jack Oliver, national finance vice chairman, Bush-Cheney 2004. Equally persuasive is the fact that Rosemary is from Chattanooga, Tennessee, so trust me, this girl knows her grits, and this girl's grits are *great*.

SERVES 6 TO 8

1½ cups grits
6 cups water
½ teaspoon salt
3 cups grated Cheddar cheese
½ stick (4 tablespoons) butter
1 clove garlic, minced
1 teaspoon Worcestershire sauce
2 eggs, beaten
Salt and pepper to taste

Preheat the oven to 350°F.

In a large saucepan, bring the grits, water, and salt to a boil, stirring constantly. Reduce the heat, cover, and simmer for 5 to 7 minutes. Add 2½ cups of the grated cheese, the butter, garlic, Worcestershire sauce, eggs, salt, and pepper. Mix together and put in a greased casserole; cover with the remaining ½ cup cheese.

Bake for 30 minutes. Or, this can be made ahead, refrigerated, and baked the day you need it.

PHIL GATES'S FRUIT BOWL DRESSING
À LA DIONNE LUCAS

Now, I know what you're thinking: Dole's Mixed Canned (not that there's anything wrong with that!), or that big glum bowl of underripe cantaloupe and strawberries that every brunch hostess feels honor-bound to provide, even if nobody really wants it. Well, Philomene Gates to the rescue. Phil, at eighty-six a practicing lawyer, civic leader, Southerner, and author (her autobiography, *A Soft Rebel Yell: From Grits to Gotham,* is a vivid read about a large and well-lived life) doesn't spend much time in the business end of the kitchen, and cheerfully admits she lifted this from the late Dionne Lucas years ago. Phil says, "This sauce brings out all the flavor of the fruit and tastes much better than a liqueur."

So cut up a bunch of colorful stuff that's in season somewhere and douse it with this dressing.

SERVES 4 TO 6

> 2 cups water
> 1 cup sugar
> Finely grated zest and juice of 2 lemons, 2 limes, and 2 oranges

In a large saucepan, boil the water with the sugar until it is reduced to about 1½ cups.

Add the citrus zest and juice to the simple syrup and simmer for 10 minutes more. Cool, and at least 30 minutes before serving, spoon over about 1 tablespoon for each cup of fruit.

NOTE: *This mixture will keep at least two months in the refrigerator, which is good news for fruit lovers and a curse for those who are not. As for me, I will try it with a little vodka and ice and let you know.*

DAD'S BAKED EGGS

'm pretty sure he invented these, but if he didn't he certainly earned the patent. Every Christmas morning for as long as I can re-member, as the family got down to the dregs of the Christmas pres-ents (ooooh, a Dust Buster! Thank you soooo much!), Dad would amble into the kitchen and start rattlin' them pots and pans. And muf-fin tins. A few more eggnogs later, we would sit down to this signature dish. Christmas of 2002 was the first time Dad wasn't there to make them, so his first grandson, my son Tim, stepped up to the plate. And the oven.

The toque is passed.

2 slices bacon per person, cooked until edible, but still very pliable
2 eggs per person, at least
Freshly ground black pepper
Minced onion (optional)
Grated Cheddar cheese (optional)
Salt
Tabasco sauce

Preheat the oven to 375°F.

Lightly butter as many muffin tins as you need to go around, even if they're nonstick. Curl a piece of bacon around the inside of each cup. Break 1 egg into each and season copiously with coarse black pepper. Sprinkle with minced onion and Cheddar, if using. Repeat until the tins are full for the number you are feeding.

Bake for 11 to 12 minutes, or until the eggs are set, but still runny inside. Remove carefully with a flexible spatula, so as not to break the yolks. Sprinkle with salt and Tabasco to taste.

Serve with onion and green pepper hash browns, sausage and yet more bacon, Entenmann's Cheese Danish and/or Raspberry and/or Lemon Coffee Cakes, and, as a sporting gesture to your aorta, a stack of whole wheat toast (see Bob Dole's Kansas Whole Wheat Honey Bread, page 117), spread with Brummel & Brown.

UNIMPEACHABLE COBBLERS,
or,
The Party's Over

...but not until you try Aunt Maxine's Old-Fashioned Vinegar Balls, Rachel's Rum Balls, Amazing Automatic Coconut Cream Pie, My Awful Ex-Sister-in-Law's Strawberry Pretzel Dessert, Jack Daniel Died for Your Sins Whiskey Cake, and Dot Czufin's Commie Pinko Carrot Cake, just to name a few.

EASY UNIMPEACHABLE PEACH COBBLER

Almost any fruit or combination can be used; blueberry is a great companion for peaches. And by the way, if you think this is easy, keep reading. The truly Republican version follows.

SERVES 8 TO 10

4 cups fresh peaches, peeled and sliced
1 cup white sugar and 1 cup brown sugar, mixed together
½ cup water
Juice of ½ juicy lemon
1 stick (8 tablespoons) unsalted butter or margarine
1½ cups all-purpose flour
3 teaspoons baking powder
1½ cups milk
Cinnamon or nutmeg to sprinkle over, if desired

Preheat the oven to 350°F.

In a saucepan, bring the peaches, 1 cup of the sugar mixture, the water, and lemon juice to a boil and let simmer for 10 minutes. Remove from the heat.

Melt the butter in 9 × 13 × 2-inch baking dish by putting it into the preheated oven.

In a medium bowl, mix together the flour, the remaining cup of the sugar mixture, the baking powder, and milk. Pour evenly into the baking dish over the melted butter, but don't stir. Spoon the fruit mixture evenly over the batter, again not stirring. Sprinkle with cinnamon or nutmeg, if using.

Bake for 30 to 40 minutes, until the batter has risen mysteriously to the top and is golden brown. Serve hot with heavy cream, whipped or not, or vanilla ice cream.

EVEN EASIER UNIMPEACHABLE PEACH COBBLER

And Even More Authentically Republican, for Reasons That Will Become Immediately Apparent, Because It Is Even More Immediately Delicious

SERVES 4, AND CAN BE DOUBLED

> 2 tablespoons butter
> 1 cup Bisquick
> ½ cup sugar
> ½ cup milk
> 3 cups thawed frozen or canned peaches

Preheat the oven to 375°F.

Melt the butter in an 8-inch square baking dish by placing it in the hot oven. In a bowl, mix the Bisquick, sugar, and milk. Pour it over the butter in the baking dish, but don't stir it into the butter. Spoon the fruit and any juices over the batter. Bake for 30 minutes.

Serve hot with heavy cream, whipped or not, or vanilla ice cream.

JACK DANIEL DIED FOR YOUR SINS
WHISKEY AND WALNUT BLACK-BOTTOM PIE

This began life as plain old pecan pie, and while there's certainly nothing wrong with that, a few tipsy tweaks here and there turn it into something pretty extraordinary.

SERVES 6 TO 8

¾ cup roughly chopped pecans
¾ cup roughly chopped walnuts, regular or black
3 eggs
½ cup dark brown sugar
1 cup dark Karo syrup
¾ stick (6 tablespoons) melted butter
1 teaspoon vanilla
¼ teaspoon salt
1 tablespoon flour
2 tablespoons or more Jack Daniel's Black Label
1 deep unbaked pie shell
Enough semisweet chocolate chips to cover the bottom of the pie
   shell (about 5 ounces)

Preheat the oven to 350°F.

Lightly skillet-toast the nuts until just beginning to brown. In a large bowl, beat the eggs and whisk in the brown sugar and Karo, then mix in the butter, vanilla, and salt. Mix the flour with the nuts, then add to the egg mixture. Stir in the Jack Daniel's.

Prick the bottom of the pie shell all over with a fork, then scatter the chocolate chips over. Pour the filling in. Bake for 35 to 45 minutes, or until the filling is puffed and a knife inserted into the middle comes out sticky but hot. The pie will continue to cook a bit after you remove it from oven. Let it cool for at least 1 hour before serving. And as long as you're in this deep, you might as well serve it with whipped or ice cream.

FROZEN PUMPKIN PIE

This is a nice spin on an old favorite for a Good Old-Fashioned Republican Thanksgiving (page 72).

SERVES 6 TO 8

1 cup cooked pumpkin (*of course* we use canned!)
1¼ cups sugar
½ teaspoon salt
½ teaspoon ground ginger
½ teaspoon ground nutmeg
1 cup whipped cream
1 baked pie shell, any kind
1 pint vanilla ice cream, softened
½ cup chopped toasted pecans (optional)

In a large bowl, combine the pumpkin, sugar, salt, and spices, mixing well, then fold in the whipped cream. Fill the bottom of the pie shell with ice cream, then top with the pumpkin–whipped cream mixture. Freeze for 2 hours or more. Top with nuts, if using, and serve.

AMAZING AUTOMATIC COCONUT CREAM PIE

I have no idea how or why this works, but it does, and deliciously.

SERVES 6 TO 8

Preheat the oven to 350°F.

Dump the following ingredients into a blender in the following order:

½ cup unsifted flour
1 cup sugar
1 cup coconut, plus a little more

Dash of salt
1½ sticks (¾ cup) butter, melted and cooled
4 eggs
2 cups milk
1 teaspoon vanilla

Turn the blender to medium for 10 seconds; then let the mixture settle for 10 seconds. Repeat 4 times, scraping down the sides of the blender as necessary. Pour into a buttered, floured 10-inch pie plate.

Bake for 1 hour, or more, until the coconut top is toasty brown.

CORN ON THE COB PIE

This one is pretty strange, but it's simpleton-simple and really, really good, and chances are nobody will guess what it is. Remember how creepy carrot cake sounded at first?

SERVES 6 TO 8

4 ears of corn (or, if it's not summer, 2 cups frozen)
3 whole eggs
One 14-ounce can condensed milk
One 12-ounce can evaporated milk (*not* fat-free; it's too late now)
1 teaspoon vanilla extract
Prepared cookie pie shell (Graham cracker or chocolate)

Preheat the oven to 350°F.

Cut the kernels off the cobs and simmer lightly in boiling water until tender (or, if using frozen, follow package directions, just don't overcook, and proceed with the recipe), then put in a blender with the eggs, both milks, and vanilla. Don't try to completely purée; the corn should (and will) be a bit piecey. Pour into the pie shell and bake for 25 to 30 minutes. Chill until firm.

A neat variation is to cook the mixture in an 8 × 12-inch baking dish instead, chill, then sprinkle brown sugar over it.

Run it under the broiler until the sugar is melted and you've got a kind of Mexican Corn Brûlée. Ole!

JACK DANIEL DIED FOR YOUR SINS WHISKEY CAKE

There's something so comforting and homey and plump and motherly about a Bundt cake—but in this case, Mother's bellying up to the bar. The first time I read this recipe I had to make it immediately. It did not disappoint.

SERVES 8 TO 10

CAKE

1 package yellow cake mix
One 3.4-ounce package instant vanilla pudding mix
¾ cup water
4 eggs
1 stick (8 tablespoons) butter, softened for creaming

WHISKEY SYRUP

1½ cups sugar
¼ cup butter
1 cup whiskey

Preheat the oven to 350°F.

Mix the cake ingredients and pour into a greased Bundt (see? Even the word is plump and motherly) pan. Bake for 55 to 60 minutes, or until a cake tester comes out clean.

Meanwhile, in a small saucepan make the whiskey syrup: heat the sugar, butter, and whiskey over low heat until clear and syrupy.

Pull the cake from the oven and while it is still hot in the pan, poke holes in it with a skewer and pour the whiskey syrup all over and through. Let the cake cool before removing it from the pan.

MY MOM'S DAY-BEFORE-YESTERDAY PINEAPPLE CHEESECAKE

Which just means this luscious cheesecake gets better with age, so make it a day or two before you plan to serve it. This was always my official birthday cake back when I used to have birthdays.

SERVES 10 TO 15

CRUST

1½ cups graham cracker crumbs, plus ½ cup extra for topping
¾ stick (6 tablespoons) butter, melted
1 tablespoon sugar

FILLING

Four 3-ounce packages cream cheese
2 eggs
½ cup sugar
½ teaspoon pure vanilla extract
2 cups crushed pineapple, drained well
Dash of cinnamon

TOPPING

1 pint sour cream
3 tablespoons sugar
1 teaspoon pure vanilla extract
Dash of cinnamon

Preheat the oven to 375°F.

Mix together 1½ cups graham cracker crumbs, butter, and sugar. Line the bottom and sides of a lavishly buttered 9-inch springform pan with the mixture, pressing to let it adhere.

With an electric mixer beat the pineapple filling ingredients, and pour into the crumb-lined pan. Bake for 20 minutes. Cool for 1 hour.

In a medium bowl, mix the topping ingredients together. Now cover with the sour cream topping and sprinkle the remaining ½ cup graham cracker crumbs over. Bake for 5 minutes more. Cool on a wire rack and then let chill for at least 1 day; 2 days are better still.

Happy birthday, Susie.

ST. BERNARD'S CHOCA-COLA CAKE

Not the St. Bernard who is the patron saint of Rémy Martin and big sweet hairy dogs, but St. Bernard as in the boys' school in Manhattan, in whose 1988 fund-raising cookbook this recipe appears. If there is a discreet, anonymous bastion of Republicanism in New York, one that quietly manages to get Republican mayors and governors (if not senators) elected in an overwhelmingly Democrat-driven state, it might be here, if you don't count a couple of the teachers.

SERVES 12 TO 16

CAKE

2 cups unbleached flour
2 cups sugar
2 sticks (1 cup) butter
3 tablespoons cocoa
1 cup Coca-Cola
1½ cups miniature marshmallows
½ cup buttermilk
2 eggs, beaten
1 teaspoon baking soda
1 teaspoon vanilla

Preheat the oven to 350°F. Grease and flour a 13 × 9 × 2-inch pan.

Combine the flour and sugar in a large bowl and set aside.

In a saucepan, place the butter and cocoa. Add the Coca-Cola and heat to boiling. Remove the mixture from the heat, add the marshmallows, and mix until dissolved. Pour the mixture over the flour and sugar and mix well. Add the buttermilk, eggs, baking soda, and vanilla and mix well. Pour into the prepared pan and bake for 45 minutes. About 5 minutes before the cake is done, quickly prepare the icing.

1 stick (8 tablespoons) butter, softened

3 tablespoons cocoa

2 tablespoons Coca-Cola

1 cup pecans or walnuts, chopped (optional, but wonderful)

One 16-ounce box of confectioners' sugar

In a saucepan, combine the butter and cocoa. Add the Coke and the nuts, if using, and heat to boiling. Pour over the sugar in a large bowl and mix well.

Ice the cake as soon as it is out of the oven. This is a tricky step; the icing seizes quickly, so it must be made at the last minute, and the point is that it sort of melts into the hot cake. Let the cake cool *thoroughly* before serving, or else you have a pudding cake—which ain't that bad, either, to tell the truth.

KAY BAILEY HUTCHISON'S FIERCELY REPUBLICAN FIRST FAMILY CAKE

They were Texas when Texas wasn't cool. Or even Texas. Kay Bailey Hutchison, the first woman senator in Texas history, is the great-great-grandaughter of Charles S. Taylor, who arrived from England in 1828, when Texas was still part of Mexico. Eight years later, he was a signer of the Texas Declaration of Independence, becoming a first citizen of what would in 1845 become the twenty-eighth state. I think. Whew. Anyway, Great-Great-Grandaddy Taylor's Taylor Family Cake was there the whole time, and it still is. Senator Hutchison explains, "This is an old-fashioned tea cake. Though the original recipe does not call for icing, I add cream cheese frosting."

¾ cup shortening

1½ cups sugar

3 eggs, beaten

1¾ cups sifted flour

½ teaspoon baking powder

½ teaspoon baking soda

½ teaspoon salt

2 teaspoons ground nutmeg

1 teaspoon ground cinnamon

¾ cup buttermilk

2 teaspoons vanilla (or 1 teaspoon vanilla and 1 teaspoon lemon extract)

1 cup coarsely chopped roasted nuts

Preheat the oven to 325°F.

In a large bowl, cream the shortening and sugar together until fluffy. Add the eggs and beat thoroughly.

Sift the dry ingredients together and add alternately with the buttermilk. Add the vanilla. Fold in the nuts. Stir the mixture well, and pour the batter into a square or round greased pan or cupcake pan. Bake for 35 to 40 minutes.

NOTE: *Caramel ice cream beaten with a little rum doesn't hurt as a topper.*

DOT CZUFIN'S COMMIE PINKO CARROT CAKE

Her voting record aside, Dot Czufin *cooked* like a Republican. Hers was the first carrot cake I ever tasted, and it is still far and away the best. This was my son's official birthday cake from the time he turned one, the year I must have been taking some funny drugs or Mommy hormones or something, for I made it in a big round pan and decorated it as a smiling cartoon lion (he's a Leo, get it?), with exquisite multicolored icings, multitextured detail, yellow-strand-by-yellow-strand mane and all. It took me hours.

Dot, on the other hand, at age eighty and long past impressing a roomful of one-year-olds, would simply throw this cake together and go into the other room with her martini and cigarette, waiting bored, for the damn thing to Just Be Done.

SERVES 12 TO 16

    1 cup salad oil
    2 cups sugar
    4 eggs
    2 cups flour
    2 teaspoons baking powder
    2 teaspoons baking soda
    1 teaspoon salt
    2 teaspoons ground cinnamon
    3 cups grated carrots
    1 cup chopped pecans or walnuts

Preheat the oven to 325°F.

Blend the salad oil and sugar in a large bowl. Add the eggs 1 at a time, beating (by hand) after each.

Sift the flour, *then* measure. Sift the rest of the dry ingredients together and add to the oil-sugar mixture. Add the carrots and nuts and mix well.

Pour into 2 large well-greased round cake pans (or 3 small ones or 2 square ones). Bake for 1 hour, or a bit more if needed. Cool.

ICING

    ½ stick (4 tablespoons) butter, at room temperature
    2 teaspoons vanilla
    1 box confectioners' sugar
    One 8-ounce package cream cheese, at room temperature

With an electric mixer, beat everything into the cream cheese.

Spread on the cooled cake and chill.

Happy birthday, Timmy.

AUNT MAXINE'S OLD-FASHIONED VINEGAR BALLS

My Aunt Maxine lives in Newburg, Missouri, population 484, where she is a tireless member of both the First Baptist Church and the Golden Girls, a popular local clogging group she founded. In the winter, she and Uncle Cecil pack up the RV they keep parked out back and head for Mission, Texas, where Aunt Maxine has founded yet another clogging group, the El Valle Cloggers, six ladies in their eighties, plus two gentlemen, who dress in homespun gingham, spangles, and taps, put on a tape of "Orange Blossom Special" or "San Antonio Rose," and clog their great big hearts out for local veterans' hospitals, nursing homes, orphanages, and other groups Desperately Seeking Diversion. I am not making this up. Proof: If you want to justify the (pitifully small) price of this book, go to www.texas-clogging.com, and you will be enormously rewarded. I think if I could be anyone else in my family besides my mother, it would be her baby sister, my Aunt Maxine.

MAKES ABOUT 20

COOK OVER MEDIUM HEAT FOR 20 MINUTES

¾ cup cider vinegar

1 cup sugar

2 cups water

1 teaspoon ground cinnamon

MAKE BALLS

2 cups flour

1 tablespoon baking powder

1 teaspoon salt

⅓ cup Crisco

¾ cup milk

Butter

¼ cup sugar combined with 2 teaspoons ground cinnamon

Preheat the oven to 375°F.

Mix well the flour, baking powder, salt, Crisco, and milk and roll into a rectangle about ¼ inch thick. Dot with butter. Sprinkle the sugar-cinnamon mixture evenly over all.

Roll up, jelly-roll style, and cut into ¼-inch slices. Place the slices cut side up close together in a deep baking dish. Pour the hot vinegar sauce over all and bake for 30 to 40 minutes, or until golden. Unbelievably good. Unbelievably.

In her own words: "This receipt here was the rage around these parts several years ago."

I love my Aunt Maxine.

RACHEL'S RUM BALLS

Rachel is the gorgeous new wife of Jack Oliver, national finance vice chairman of Bush-Cheney 2004, making these rum balls, even if they did not include rum, very Republican indeed. Luckily, they do include rum, and enough to get your attention. These are luscious and lethal, and after a few of them even Ted Kennedy might feel like writing a nice big fat check.

MAKES 4 DOZEN

> One 6-ounce package (1 cup) semisweet chocolate pieces
> ½ cup sugar, plus more for rolling balls in
> ⅓ cup dark rum
> 3 tablespoons light corn syrup
> 2 cups crushed vanilla wafers (measure after crushing)
> 1 cup ground walnuts or pecans

In a saucepan, melt the chocolate pieces over low heat, carefully. Remove from the heat. Stir in ½ cup sugar, the rum, and corn syrup. Fold in the vanilla wafers and nuts. Shape the dough into 1-inch balls, 2 teaspoons for each. Roll in more sugar. Chill. Store in an airtight container unless, of course, you just eat the whole 4 dozen right there, sparing yourself the trouble of finding that darned airtight container.

HEAVENLY HEATH BAR CRACKER COOKIES

As in dying and going to.

MAKES 35, BUT DON'T INVITE 34 OTHER PEOPLE JUST YET

35 saltine crackers (which is one sleeve, did you know that?)
3 sticks (1½ cups) unsalted butter
1½ cups packed light brown sugar
1 teaspoon vanilla or almond extract
One 11½-ounce package milk chocolate chips
One half 10-ounce package Hershey's toffee bits

Preheat the oven to 400°F. Line a 15 × 10-inch jelly-roll pan with aluminum foil, and lightly oil with vegetable oil.

Place the saltines, salt side up, in the pan (they should cover the bottom of the pan). Boil the butter and brown sugar in a saucepan for 2 or 3 minutes, stirring so it doesn't burn. Remove from the heat and stir in the extract. Pour the sugar mixture all over the saltines and bake for 3 to 5 minutes, or until hot and bubbly. Remove from the oven and, while still very hot, lay the chocolate pieces over, covering, then the toffee bits, then just stand there, drooling, watching everything melt. If it's not happening fast enough, stick it all back in the oven until it is good and gooey. If you can bear it, cool until hard, break into saltine-shaped squares (they are already pre-scored, which is nice, but unimportant), and eat.

NOTE: *I do not mind telling you these are pretty good hot and just-melted, too, which reminds me, you can always put the cooled ones in the microwave, remelt, and serve with ice cream. No jury would convict you.*

ALICE HANDLEY'S PEARLY GATES PRALINE GRAHAMS

A variation on the Heavenly Heath Bar Cracker Cookies (see above), and equally insanely simple and divine.

Graham crackers, enough to line the bottom of a jelly-roll pan
2 sticks (1 cup) butter or margarine
1 cup brown sugar
1 cup chopped pecans

Preheat the oven to 350°F.

Fill the bottom of a foil-lined and greased baking pan with graham crackers.

Boil the butter and brown sugar for 4 minutes, stir in the pecans, and spread over the graham crackers. Bake for 8 to 10 minutes. Let cool before serving.

SCOTCH SQUARES

Oddly enough for a Republican recipe, I don't mean that kind of scotch.

MAKES 16 SQUARES

$\frac{1}{3}$ cup butter
$\frac{1}{3}$ cup brown sugar, packed
1 cup flour
$\frac{1}{2}$ cup chopped nuts
$\frac{1}{4}$ cup sugar
One 8-ounce package cream cheese, softened
1 egg
2 tablespoons milk
1 tablespoon fresh lemon juice
$\frac{1}{2}$ teaspoon vanilla

Preheat the oven to 350°F.

In a large bowl, combine the butter and brown sugar and cream until light. Add the flour and nuts and mix until crumbly. Measure 1 cup of the mixture and set aside, to use for topping later. Press the remaining mixture into an 8-inch square pan and bake for 15 minutes.

With an electric mixer beat the sugar and cream cheese until smooth, then add the egg, milk, lemon juice, and vanilla and beat for

1 minute. Spread the cheese mixture over the baked crust and sprinkle on the reserved topping. Bake for 25 minutes. Cool and cut into 2-inch squares.

MARCY GARKIE'S CHERRY DESSERT

Marcy Garkie lives in Orange County, proud home of John Wayne International Airport. Need I say more?

Incidentally, this has proven to be one of the most wildly successful recipes in this book. I have never had leftovers, including, humiliatingly, the time I made it just for myself. And I wasn't even pregnant.

SERVES 8 TO 10

Preheat the oven to 350°F.
In a greased 9 × 12-inch baking pan, layer

One 21-ounce can cherry pie filling
One 20-ounce can slightly drained crushed pineapple
1 package yellow cake mix
1½ sticks (12 tablespoons) butter, melted
1½ cups chopped pecans

Bake for 45 minutes, and serve hot with ice cream or heavy cream. In the privacy of your own bedroom.

NOTE: *A terrific variation is blueberry pie filling, lemon cake mix, and chopped almonds. Less sweet, and even better when cooled and set.*

MY AWFUL EX-SISTER-IN-LAW'S STRAWBERRY PRETZEL DESSERT

I do not recall who gave me this recipe, I don't, honest I don't, come on, I said I don't, didn't I? But in defense of the awful ex-sister-in-law, whoever she is, this is so good, how bad could she have been?

SERVES 6 TO 8

> 2 cups crushed pretzels
> 1½ sticks (¾ cup) melted butter
> 1 cup plus 3 tablespoons sugar
> One 8-ounce package cream cheese, softened
> 2 cups Cool Whip, plus more if desired
> One 6-ounce package strawberry Jell-O
> 2 cups boiling water
> Two 10-ounce packages frozen strawberries

Preheat the oven to 400°F.

Make the crust: Combine the pretzels, butter, and 3 tablespoons of the sugar and line a buttered 9 × 13-inch pan with the mixture. Bake for 5 minutes. Let cool.

Make the filling: Mix the cream cheese, the remaining 1 cup of sugar, and the Cool Whip. Spread onto the crust, making sure the edges are sealed. Refrigerate until chilled. Mix the Jell-O and boiling water until the Jell-O is dissolved, and let cool slightly. Add the strawberries, pour over the cream cheese layer, and chill until the Jell-O is set. Cut into squares and serve with more topping, if desired.

AUNT EMMY'S BLEEDING HEART BROWNIES

(Using Her Mother's Advice)

Aunt Emmy, in 1942 a PFC in the newly minted United States Navy WAVES, was, thirty-eight years later, an alternate delegate to the 1980 Democratic Convention here in New York. She stayed with me, arriving warily at my Republican apartment wearing all her Jimmy Carter stuff, like a virgin wearing garlic and a crucifix to ward off vampires. She was also wearing her famous JANE WYMAN WAS RIGHT button, and, I swear, she still does, twenty-four years after Ronald Reagan's landslide. Talk about denial. Anyway, Aunt Emmy's cooking philosophy is derived from her mother and is as follows: "If it comes in a box or a can and is easy, don't be a fool. USE IT."

MAKES 1 DOZEN

> 1 large box brownie mix

Follow the directions on the box for cakelike brownies. Cool slightly, then spread peanut butter (creamy or chunky) over the top and cool some more.

In a saucepan, mix ¼ cup each oleo (*sic*), cocoa, and milk plus 1 cup sugar. Bring to a rolling boil and boil for 1 minute. Place the pan in cold water and add 1 teaspoon vanilla. After cooling for a few minutes, beat with a mixer until spreadable. Now pour it over the peanut butter bit. *Instantly!* Or it will be too late.

IN HER OWN WORDS: *"If you're lucky, the fudge topping will set well. On the other hand, there may be a time when it doesn't. You can't win them all."*

NANCY LINDSAY'S SPOTTED DICK NIXON

Nancy Lindsay is the Sweetheart of the Westminster Kennel Club, a frequent Best in Show judge, and a founder of the Museum of the Dog in St. Louis, Missouri. You didn't know there was a dog museum? Well, you should, because it is one of the most elegant little (and little-known) museums in the country. Go. It is wonderful. Nancy's husband, Roddy, is the baby brother of the late John Lindsay, who, in 1964, became the first Republican mayor of New York City since Fiorello La Guardia. She makes this pudding in honor of the Lindsay Scottish genes and because she likes to say "Spotted Dick Nixon."

A little warmed maple syrup over the pudding isn't bad either, nor is just plain old heavy whipping cream.

10 ounces sweet suet pastry (recipe follows)
4 ounces raisins or currants
Grated zest of 1 lemon
Custard Sauce (recipe follows)

Roll out the pastry into a strip about 10 inches long and ¾ inch thick. Lay the raisins over the pastry, leaving a ½-inch margin all around; press the raisins in lightly and sprinkle with the lemon zest. Moisten the edges and roll up from one of the long sides, forming a log; seal the edges firmly and roll in a floured pudding cloth or cheesecloth. Make a pleat in the cloth to allow the pastry to expand, and tie the ends firmly. Boil or steam for 1½ hours and serve with the Custard Sauce.

SWEET SUET PASTRY

1 pound all-purpose flour
6 ounces caster sugar, the brown British kind (or steal packets of Sugar in the Raw from Starbucks), or just use regular granulated
1 ounce baking powder
½ pound finely chopped suet with skin
1 cup whole milk

In a bowl, mix the ingredients to form a stiff dough.

CUSTARD SAUCE

1½ cups whole milk
6 large egg yolks
⅓ cup sugar
Pinch of salt

Bring the milk just to a boil in a heavy 3-quart saucepan and remove from the heat. Whisk together the yolks, sugar, and salt in a bowl and start adding the hot milk, whisking. Pour the custard into the pan and cook over moderately low heat, stirring constantly, until slightly thickened. Pour into a pitcher and serve over the pudding.

INDEX

vermouth, in The General's Instant Martini, 4
vinaigrettes:
  Maple Syrup, Dee Austin's, 35
  Sherry, 34
Vinegar Balls, Old-Fashioned, Aunt Maxine's, 140–41
vodka:
  The Big Appletini, 4–5
  The Calvin Cooler, 5–6
  Martini, Instant, The General's, 4
  The Salty Yaller Dawg, 6–7

walnut(s):
  Bleu Tippecanoes with Sherry Vinaigrette, Maya Schaper's, 33–34
  Rosemary's, 11
  and Whiskey Black-Bottom Pie, Jack Daniel Died for Your Sins, 131
water chestnuts, in Evelyn Grayson's Foo Yung Toss, 40–41
Westminster Kennel Club, 146
whiskey:
  Cake, Jack Daniel Died for Your Sins, 134
  Margarita, Dad's, 10
  Old-Fashioned, A Good Old-Fashioned Republican, 6

and Walnut Black-Bottom Pie, Jack Daniel Died for Your Sins, 131
White Bean Chili, Sandy Berkeley's, 89–90
Whole Wheat Honey Bread, Kansas, Bob Dole's, 117
wild rice:
  Pancakes with Smoked Trout and Horseradish Cream, The Unsinkable Annie Gunn's, 123–25
  Sausage, with Cherries, Soozy's Boozy, 70
William Least Heat-Moon's Pappy Van Winkle on the Rocks, 7–8
World's Best Slaw, 101–2
Wyman, Jane, 145–46

yaller-dawg Democrat, 6
yellow summer squash, in Section Four Summer Squash, 105–6
Yogurt Sauce, 84–85

Zabriski, Mary, 20
Ziff, Magi Durham, 109–10
Zorba the Shrimp, 45–46
zucchini, in Section Four Summer Squash, 105–6

SUSANNE GRAYSON TOWNSEND is a New York City Republican.

We'll pause here for a moment while that sinks in.

She is also a recovering advertising executive who woke up one morning and realized she had spent most of her adult life teaching America how to unscrew their Oreos ("A Kid'll Eat the Middle of an Oreo First . . ."); persuading women that Clairol Balsam Color gave them Big, Fat, Beeyootiful Hair; and that Chameleon Sunglasses could Change Your Whole Outlook (but Serengeti Sunglasses would Arouse Your Animal Instincts); and once, in London, convincing much of Western Europe that Schweppes was the Great British Schhhhhhound. On behalf of clients ranging from Nestlé to Noxell, Purina to Ponds, Bermuda to Bristol-Meyers, Colgate to Corning, Anheuser-Busch to AOL, J&J to Frito-Lay, she had put words into the mouths of royalty (the Duchess of York, B.B. King, and Aretha Franklin, the Queen of Soul), the sublime (Bobby Short, Gladys Knight, Lauren Hutton, Bart Starr, Bart Simpson), and the ridiculous (Cousin Minnie Pearl, Linda Evans). Moreover, she had actually been paid for these shenanigans by such esteemed advertising agencies as Foote, Cone & Belding, the legendary William Esty Company, and various venues within the Interpublic Group of Companies. She had won Clios, Andys, an Addy, a Cannes lion, many inclusions in *Ad Age*'s 100 Best and the International Broadcast Awards, and, one particularly proud year, a Distinguished Achievement Award from the National Association to Aid Fat Americans.

Was that all there was?

That's when she decided it was time to do something real, something meaningful, something for her spirit and her legacy, something for her fellow man and woman, something that might get her into *The New York Times* without paying when she died. In short, it was time to write *How to Eat Like a Republican*.

So much for epiphanies.

ABOUT THE ILLUSTRATOR

TONY ZAMORA'S uncle was a famous cel animator with Disney in the 1930s. So it came as no surprise when Tony, lifelong visions of Pinocchio and Snow White and the Seven Dwarfs dancing in his head, applied for a full cartoonist scholarship at New York's prestigious School of Visual Arts. Confidently assuming that the Disney DNA made him a lock, he was poised and relaxed.

"Where do I sign?" he inquired politely.

"Do you do anything else?" SVA inquired politely back.

"Ahh, well, I do have an advertising portfolio," he stammered.

"That's good."

Many years and many award-winning advertising campaigns later—MasterCard, Myers's Rum, Quaker Oats, to name a very few—Tony has decided it is time to bust out of Madison Avenue's closet and dive back into his illustration gene pool. The eagle has landed.

And landed deliciously on *How to Eat Like a Republican*.

The author is grateful beyond words.